The Best
Men's Stage Monologues
# of 2003

Smith and Kraus *Books for Actors*
MONOLOGUE AUDITION SERIES
The Best Men's / Women's Stage Monologues of 2002
The Best Men's / Women's Stage Monologues of 2001
The Best Men's / Women's Stage Monologues of 2000
The Best Men's / Women's Stage Monologues of 1999
The Best Men's / Women's Stage Monologues of 1998
The Best Men's / Women's Stage Monologues of 1997
The Best Men's / Women's Stage Monologues of 1996
The Best Men's / Women's Stage Monologues of 1995
The Best Men's / Women's Stage Monologues of 1994
The Best Men's / Women's Stage Monologues of 1993
The Best Men's / Women's Stage Monologues of 1992
The Best Men's / Women's Stage Monologues of 1991
The Best Men's / Women's Stage Monologues of 1990
One Hundred Men's / Women's Stage Monologues from the 1980s
2 Minutes and Under: Character Monologues for Actors Volumes I and II
Monologues from Contemporary Literature: Volume I
Monologues from Classic Plays 468 BC to 1960 AD
100 Great Monologues from the Renaissance Theatre
100 Great Monologues from the Neo-Classical Theatre
100 Great Monologues from the 19th Century Romantic and Realistic Theatres
The Ultimate Audition Series Volume I: 222 Monologues, 2 Minutes & Under
The Ultimate Audition Series Volume II: 222 Monologues, 2 Minutes & Under
     from Literature

YOUNG ACTOR MONOLOGUE SERIES
Cool Characters for Kids: 71 One-Minute Monologues
Great Scenes and Monologues for Children, Volumes I and II
Great Monologues for Young Actors, Volumes I and II
Short Scenes and Monologues for Middle School Actors
Multicultural Monologues for Young Actors
The Ultimate Audition Series for Middle School Actors Vol.I: 111 One-Minute
     Monologues
The Ultimate Audition Series for Teens Vol. I: 111 One-Minute Monologues
The Ultimate Audition Series for Teens Vol.II: 111 One-Minute Monologues
The Ultimate Audition Series for Teens Vol.III: 111 One-Minute Monologues
The Ultimate Audition Series for Teens Vol.IV: 111 One-Minute Monologues
The Ultimate Audition Series for Teens Vol.V: 111 One-Minute Monologues
     from Shakespeare
Wild and Wacky Characters for Kids: 60 One-Minute Monologues

If you require prepublication information about upcoming Smith and Kraus books, you may receive our semiannual catalogue, free of charge, by sending your name and address to *Smith and Kraus Catalogue, PO Box 127, Lyme, NH 03768. Or call us at (800) 895-4331; fax (603) 643-6431.*

The Best
Men's Stage Monologues
of 2003

edited by D. L. Lepidus

MONOLOGUE AUDITION SERIES

A SMITH AND KRAUS BOOK

Published by Smith and Kraus, Inc.
177 Lyme Road, Hanover, NH 03755
www.SmithKraus.com

First Edition: April 2004
10 9 8 7 6 5 4 3 2 1

Cover illustration by Lisa Goldfinger
Cover design by Julia Hill Gignoux

The Monologue Audition Series
ISSN 1067-134X
ISBN 1-57525-334-8

NOTE: These monologues are intended to be used for audition and class study; permission is not required to use the material for those purposes. However, if there is a paid performance of any of the scenes included in this book, please refer to the permissions acknowledgment pages 99–102 to locate the source that can grant permission for public performance.

Contents

Foreword

Two years ago, when Marisa Smith asked me to take over Smith and Kraus' exemplary series of monologue books, I thought, "What an honor!" Little did I imagine what a daunting task this would be, reading through hundreds of plays each year, on the lookout for the best, the most useful, monologues for class or audition use; or, just-as-daunting, procuring all the rights required to put these monologues in this book. But when I think of just how useful this book is going to be to you (or, if you are a teacher, to your students), it makes it all worthwhile.

In this book you will find a wide variety of characters, of various ages (though I included as many monologues as I could find age-appropriate for younger performers, under forty). You will find a wide variety of styles. You will recognize many of the plays, small excerpts from which I have included here, and many of the playwrights; but many of these writers will be new to you. Almost all of the monologues herein are from published, readily available plays. In the case of those from unpublished manuscripts, I have included in the rights pages in the back of this book information as to how you can contact the author directly, so that you may procure the complete text. Check out the rights pages, as well, for information on which publisher has published which play.

To my disappointment, I was unable to get rights to some other fine pieces, for one reason or another. Elaine May's *Taller Than a Dwarf* and *Adult Entertainment* have some fine monologues, as do Edward Albee's *The Goat* and Peter Gaitens' *Flesh and Blood*, to name but a few. I recommend all these plays to your attention as well.

In closing, I wish to express my gratitude to those authors, agents, and publishers who understand that these monologue books are a great way to put the word out about new plays, and that they provide a vital service to actors and acting students, which is why they have graciously allowed me to put their terrific pieces in this book. Thanks, too, to Marisa Smith, Eric Kraus, Julia Gignoux, and intern Erin Meanley, all of whose assistance was invaluable.

I hope you find That Perfect Monologue in this book. If you don't, check out Smith and Kraus' monologue books from other years — particularly, the ones I edited.

D.L. Lepidus

Actor!
Frederick Stroppel

Comic

Actor (here, a kid)

> This play is a hilarious, surreal satire spoofing the actor's life, following it from birth to death. Here, the young actor is about to make his first performance.

ACTOR: An actor? Who respects actors? All they do is make believe. (*The actor slips on a robe and a bejeweled turban.*) I mean, this is just silly. Look how supremely foolish I appear. And all those parents and teachers out there are supposed to believe I'm from a different time, a different culture, a different world, just because I say so? I just can't take it seriously, I'm sorry. This can't be a man's work, to pose and pretend and . . .
>   (*Spotlight hits actor. He immediately reacts, and he goes into his speech with shaky confidence.*)
>   "I, too, have followed the star to this poor babe's stable." (*The spotlight goes off. Excited:*) My God! That was incredible! All alone, just me, in front of all those people. And they were listening! I could feel it! I *moved* them. Lord, I'm getting chills! I want to do that again! I can't wait till tomorrow! But tomorrow will be better. This was only a surface reading. I have to get under the skin off my character. Who is Gaspar? Was he a tall man, did he stoop? Where did he glom all this frankincense? Did he convert, or was this just a one-time fling? So many questions! Please, leave me alone! I need my space right now! I owe this time to my muse! Concentrate, be the center within this center, find the zone . . . (*Spotlight hits the actor again. This time he steps forward, takes a measured pause, milks the moment for its drama.*) "I, too, have followed the star to this poor stabe's bable." (*Spotlight off. Elated:*) Wow! I got a laugh, and I wasn't even trying! I'm a natural! The stage is my home! I have found my purpose on Earth!

Actor!
Frederick Stroppel

Comic

Teacher (any age)

> *Actor!* is a hilarious, surreal satire on the actor's life. Here, a cynical acting teacher rants about what a crummy life that is.

Acting School. The teacher is holding forth on the mystery of acting.

TEACHER: So what is acting? Is it the art of Make-believe, or is it the expression of Truth? Or both, or neither? And by extension, what then is the actor? Is he sorcerer, wizard, necromancer? Or rather prophet, Cassandra, relentless foe of hypocrisy? Are we escaping reality in the theater, or rushing toward it? These are vast, imponderable matters, and frankly they have as much relevance to your situation as a vat of Tibetan monk shit! *(Pacing, with controlled sarcasm.)* You all want to be famous actors, is that it? And you think I can help you? You think I can put you on the road to stardom? Well now, don't you think if I *knew* how to be a famous actor, I would *be* a famous actor? Don't you think I would take advantage of my own mystical wisdom and catapult myself into the stratified realm of twenty-million-dollar salaries and development deals, instead of standing in this squalid, airless closet, pontificating for a percentage of your meager wages? Some of you are fresh from your latest college or high school triumph, and you're ready to "conquer the big city." Fat fucking chance, my friends. Whether you played George Gibbs or Billy Bigelow or John Gabriel Borkman, you'll never play that character again, or anything close. Your stardom is over. There may be one person in this class — *one* — worthy of a leading role, and he's not going to get it, either, because it's going to go to some untrained mush-mouthed movie-star punk with half a beard and a thriving drug dependency. From now on, you'll be Joe the Used-Car Salesman; Cop

Number Three; The Blonde Extra in the Bikini. That's right, ladies, check your cellulite at the door. You won the Drama Award back in Poughkeepsie? Well, now you have to learn how to act with your ass — that's the side of your personality most likely to see the camera. Am I making myself clear to you people? Talent means nothing! Your chance of success in this chosen field ranges from zero to nil! — unless of course you went to Yale. For the better part of your adult life you will be scratching and clawing your way to the lower half of the middle! Along the way you will shed your income, your future, and your self-respect! Ninety-nine point nine percent of you are on a treadmill to nowhere.

Appointment with a Highwire Lady
Russell Davis

Dramatic

Richard (twenties)

> Richard has had a breakdown and is in a mental institution. He has lost his sense of touch, his focus, and he has a tenuous grip on reality. He is here talking to Louise, a friend from his past, who has come to try and save him.

RICHARD: I paid somebody in town. To let me keep it in town. And I used to sneak down and ride it. It was a secret even from you. Because the first thing I wanted to do in my life was to play soccer. To go to Europe and play soccer. On an Italian team. But there was a second thing growing. Which was to ride a motorcycle. To race it. *(Pause.)* And when I took you on the motorcycle, it was this night. In the photograph. I think it was the photograph, later. And I didn't plan to go so fast. I started fast, but that was just showing off. I was showing what I practiced. That's all. And you knew that too. Because I could feel you trusting me. You were trusting and holding onto my back. Like my back was broad. It was a big wall, a protection, between you and anything that could happen to you no matter what was ahead of us in this world. And there was nothing that could equal the feeling. The trust I felt you had in me.

> And then I found these grooves in my mind. I had been looking for these grooves. And I put my mind in each groove and it took us up and down the mountain, the mountain roads, like a centripetal force. Everything was guided. It was in a groove. But then I began to understand there is an edge to each groove. *(Rises from his chair.)* You can't go to an even further edge. And I wanted so bad to go to

4

this edge. I wanted to step off. Because I saw this edge in front of us and I knew we could step off. I knew we could do it together.

And then I felt you. I felt you slamming your head into my back. I could hear you pulling on my hair with your hand and screaming to me to stop. I felt you ripping the skin of my cheek off. *(Pause.)* And I think it was a miracle we did stop. That the bike flew away from my legs, and my hands, it left my control. And we slid on my back, somehow up a hill.

But that changed me. And it changed you. Because you knew I could kill you. And I would kill myself. You could see this hole. You knew I could go down the hole. *(Sinks to the floor.)* That's why I remember your face. I remember when we got up from the motorcycle. And you looked at me from your face. *(Pause.)* So this is me now. I'm in a room now. And I think all the things I did before I came to this room were just a trick. To take up time. Make activity. A trick that didn't work to keep from coming to this room. *(Pause.)* Because this is my room. A white room. I have belonged in this room. I have belonged to come to a place where walls can move, and nothing is even. *(Pause.)* What I don't think belongs to me. What I didn't know. Was that you could visit. You could still visit. Even after you saw.

And I am very grateful. You cannot know. You cannot know, how after all these things, I did not know we could still have this visit. . . .

I hit Malcolm Cribbs because according to him our lives are like the universe. They scatter and spread out. All the events kept getting farther and farther from each other. The memories. Just spread out. Accelerate. Till we get to the end, the outer reaches, and we're so thin and spread out and that's it. We have to die. Because there's nothing left that can handle the distances between the events in our lives.

That is what Malcolm Cribbs has to say about life. When it is normal. But he also thinks he is an expert when it is not normal. He has told me the reverse of this theory of losing gradual focus and dying. He has said there is an opposite. There are some of us who don't die. We don't spread out. Which is a black hole. We are like a black hole. All events happen so fast, we don't know how to put distance between them, they happen too fast, and so they pile up on top of each other. They jam all together until you are confronted with this big black ball, this thing with no handles in it, this concentration of memory, time is bent, space, and this thing drags you in and you accelerate, you keep going in, you keep crushing, until you smash right inside. *(Pause.)* That is why I hit Malcolm Cribbs. Because he makes me think I am a thing nobody can untangle. Or do anything about. Like death. People ignore me, like death, to get on with their lives. *(Pause.)* What did we used to do together?

Beauty's Daughter
Dael Orlandersmith

Seriocomic

Papo (seventeen)

> Papo, a Puerto Rican teenager from the Lower East Side, NYC, has
> come to Diane's house to plead with her to write a school paper,
> which is due in two days.

PAPO: Yo. You wouldn't want to ruin the potential of a future genius. *(Beat.)*
See, I know you can write that shit and hook it up, so it'll be real
dope. *(Beat.)* What you writin' here — let me see. Check it out.
(Bends over as if reading something on her desk.) "I touched the shoes
of Mary Magdalene on Avenue D." Yo, Diane, that shit is fly — See,
c'mon mommy, write my paper for me. See if you bring that kinda
poetic justice, yo, my shit will be hooked up, and I promise, yo, not
to do this shit again 'cause I know the only person I'm cheatin' is
myself. *(Beat.)* See, next time, I'll hook it up, so that I have saved
enough loot and I can quit scrambling and just do my schoolwork.
'Cause yo, I care about my future. *(Beat.)* See, let me tell you what
I plan on doin' — check this out, I'll attend college in about a year,
a year and a half, no later. See after I graduate high school 'cause even
though I wanna cut back on dealin', yo, I gotta be realistic, yo, I gotta
scramble like twice a week 'cause like I said, my pops is buggin' out
on Bacardi all the time now! And also before I go away I gotta make
sure he don't hit my moms and sisters no more. See I can't be self-
ish, y'know. *(Pause.)* Sometimes, right, like even though something
may be wrong — Like I know dealing weed is wrong — Like you
gotta realize that the money I make is helpin' out, y'know? See Diane,
sometimes you gotta do certain things 'cause you know eventually
it may pay off and help someone in the long run, right? *(Beat.)* Like
you doin' my paper — yo, like that right? I mean how many times
can I tell you, that although I fucked up — unintentionally — that

my future is in your hands. Say what? I know you ain't callin' me a punk. *(Pause.)* Diane, de que? Lissen, Diane — I don't let nobody call me that. Know what I'm saying? Yo, I don't like that shit. *(Pause.)* I'm a punk 'cause I can't leave? That's my family. Yo, I can't turn my back on my family like that. *(Pause.)* Yo, no matter how bad they are, they're still my blood — you don't turn your back on your own, man. Yo, I'm not you. I can't do that! The last time he beat her, man, he kicked her like she was a dog, I grabbed that motherfucker and said, "Hit her again, and I'll ram my shank up your ass." Diane, man, I'm beggin' you please, yo please. Yo, I'll never ask you to do this again. *(Crosses his heart.)* I swear to God! Diane, remember, what did you say to me? You said, "Papo you got to make your life better and ain't nobody gonna give you shit. If you don't create a life for yourself, on your own terms, your life is not gonna amount to anything." *(Pause.)* Huh? You're disappointed in me? Yo, you disappointed in me? Well, I'm pretty disappointed in you too! Like you and me supposed to be friends and yo, you give me back when I need you. How do you think that makes me feel? Well, dat's what I'm trying to do Diane. Mommy please. So what do you say? I fucked up? Lissen you know what? I'm leavin' your house. Yo, I already know I can't be all that anyway — writing books? Yo, that's bullshit — I'm leavin OK? Sorry to bother you. Fuck it, I'm gone. *(He exits.)*

Black Thang

Ato Essandoh

Comic

Jerome (black, twenties to thirties)

> Jerome is talking to his best friend Sam, who has recently started dating a white woman (Sam, like Jerome, is black). Jerome is "educating" him about why he's made the right choice.

JEROME: See that's the great thing with white chicks. You ain't gotta have money, you ain't gotta have a job, education, you ain't gotta have shit. Just a big dick and a smile and if they like you, they'll fuck you. You know what I mean? All I gotta say is . . . Once you go white . . . You do it for spite! Fuck sisters man. Too much work. Too much drama. Baby Daddy's pounding on your door at three in the morning. *(Mimicking "Baby Daddy.")* "A yo! Shaneequa! I know you in there!" Fuck that shit. White girls? No muss, no fuss. Just handle your business in the dicking department and they'll buy you shit, cook for you, take care of you. Plus they can hail you a cab anytime you want man. What more do you need?

Yo know what your problem is man?

Lack of ambition. You're not seeing the big picture my friend. This is not about you and one white chick. This is about you and all the white chicks. This is God saying, "Go forth my son and plunder the white man's natural resources." You owe it to yourself. You owe it to us. Power to the people! That's what I'm talking about. I mean look at you man. Ya fine-ass Mandigo-looking motherfucker. How are you not fucking every minute of the day? I mean you're so good-looking I'd fuck you. And I don't mean that in the gay way. I mean it in the prison way. If we were in lockdown, I'd be fucking the shit outta you right now. Shit I'd let you fuck me. That's how good-looking you are.

Black Thang
Ato Essandoh

Comic

Jerome (twenties to thirties)

> Jerome, a black guy, is talking to his friend Sam, another black guy,
> recounting the story of an encounter with an Indian woman he met
> at a sneaker store. Sam and Jerome have had a falling out of their
> friendship as a result of a conflict over a woman both fell for. This
> is Jerome's attempt at an apology.

JEROME: I knew this Indian chick once. You know, red dot on the fore-
head and all that shit. Her name was Sipi. Worked at the Foot Locker
on Flatbush. She was something. Mad cute in the umpire strips. Little black Converse on. That girl was fine man. Fine ass little Sipi.
Sold me a pair of Airwalks, the New Jordans when they came out.
A pair of Reebok pumps. Remember Reebok pumps? The fly shit.
Right? Sold me all kinds of shit. Socks, Ts, my Knicks hat. Damn,
I would just go in there sometimes, not even wanting to buy shit.
Just check her out. She had this shy smile, the way she looked at me,
all shy and shit. I think she was sweating me too. You know. So one
time I'm like, "Yo check this out, I'ma roll up in there and ask for
her number, and I'ma take her to Coney Island." You know, go slow
because you could tell that she was one of those slow girls. Take a
whole six months before she'll let you even see her bra strap you know
what I'm saying? Probably got to go to some funky ass holy temple
and sacrifice a goat or some shit before she'll let you fuck her. You
know what I mean? But she looked like she was worth it. You know
them Indian people be some freaks behind closed doors. Kama Sutra?
'Nuff said. So I rolled up in there, had my pumps on, had my Knicks
hat on with matching Reebok suit. Yeah, you know the deal. And I
rolled up in there and I said "A yo Sipi come here girl!" And she was
all embarrassed and shit. Talking about "Can I help you sir?" And I

was like "Yeah you can help me . . . what's up with that red dot on your forehead girl somebody poke you or what?" You know, just trying to break the ice and shit. And she looked at me for a second . . . and started to cry. And I'm like "Naw Sipi baby don't cry I was just teasing. Shit I like the red dot!" And that was the truth. I was cool with the red dot. But she just kept crying like I stole her suede Pumas or something. So the manager, probably her father or some shit comes out and says to me *(Mimicking Indian manager.)* "My friend. You must leave. You must leave right now my friend." And I'm like: "Yo can't I apologize? Can I say I'm sorry?" "No my friend you must leave. You must leave right now my friend. Or I call the cops." Shit what's this friend shit? You ain't my friend motherfucker! You ain't my friend! How are you gonna call the cops on your friend? So anyway, they kicked me out. Banned me from Foot Locker. Imagine that? Ban a brother from Foot Locker? That shit ain't right . . . I heard through the Foot Locker grapevine that Sipi went to med school a couple of years ago. I knew that girl was smart. Heard she got married too. Some Indian doctor. Two doctors in the house? They must be making bank! Wish I could see her again. Let her know I was cool with the red dot.

The Boys They Left Behind
Donald Steele

Dramatic

Jack (thirties to forties)

> Jack plays a doctor on a TV soap opera. He is talking to his brother
> Brian, who is a real doctor and who can't stand him. The doctor he
> is referring to was their father's doctor. Their father has recently passed
> away.

JACK: Actually I thought Dr. Jarid was pretty demeaning the way he kept
calling me "doctor" or "doc" and asking me for a second opinion.
Oh he did it with a smile and a nudge in my side with his elbow
but right behind those shiny capped teeth of his I could hear him
hissing "Actor. Actor. Phony. Actor." I *did* tell him. I *did* tell him he
should consult you. Maybe he would have if someone other than an
actor had suggested it, he'd have listened. If I sold real estate. If I
was a banker. Even a bank teller. Or a janitor at the bank. But no.
You were being recommended by an actor. What's that? That's not
a real job. Acting? That's why Dad liked me so much. He thought
I was pulling the wool over everyone's eyes making so much money
and not really doing a real job to get that much money. What a scam.
Those first years when my whole summer salary at one of those barn
theaters wouldn't even amount to my per diem today, Dad thought
I was a fool. And said so. It wasn't til the TV stuff started coming in
that he had a change of heart. I still wasn't the real thing. But the
money I made, that was the real thing. Except it was money for doing
nothing is how he saw it. So no matter how good I did, he still
thought he had it all over me. Cause he had a real job. A man's job.

The Boys They Left Behind
Donald Steele

Dramatic

Brian (thirties to forties)

> Brian, a doctor, is talking to his brother Jack, a soap opera actor, whom he can't stand. The two brothers are meeting in what was their family home after the death of a parent.

BRIAN: It doesn't have to be interesting to me. You're the one . . . *(Pause.)* doing it. *(Pause.)* I'm married to who I'm married to because I don't have that much expected of me. Make sure we speak every few days when she's teaching out of town or I'm at a conference somewhere. Show up from time to time at one of her poetry readings. Be there when she has a book signing. She doesn't even expect me to read what she's written. She understands. I'm too busy. I have enough expected of me in my professional life. I can only take so much obligation. I'm married to someone who has a big full life of her own and I don't have to supply her with that much. I'm supportive hell yes. We understand each other's lives. We make room in our lives for each other. But I didn't want to be what someone did with her life. I certainly didn't want a wife like our mother was. So I married Nancy and was perpetually angry with her that I wasn't her whole life, her every waking minute. And then after the divorce and enough therapy, I was ready for someone who I wasn't always angry at for being like our mother and angry at because she wasn't like our mother. And with Maxine, I have that. I've learned what I can handle. What I can have. How much I can be for someone. But there is a part of me that does want to be someone's whole life, that does want to be someone's every waking minute. I would like to think I could be that much for somebody. That if I disappeared, part of them would disappear too. Part of them would be gone too. They'd be missing a part of themselves if I weren't there.

Broadway Macabre

Don Nigro

Seriocomic

Old Producer (old)

The Old Producer — an old man with white hair, pale, skeletal — sits in an armchair and speaks to a young playwright whose play he is trying to produce. The Producer looks and speaks like a gentleman, so that when he bursts out with obscenities it's particularly striking, because of the great contrast to the courtly demeanor he's cultivated all his life. In fact he is the son of a poor Jewish immigrant who spent his youth hawking tickets on Broadway, and he has clawed his way to the top over a period of fifty or sixty years. He is a very tough old bird, with a sense of humor, a terrible temper that bursts out and then subsides again, a dark fatalism, and a powerful will to conquer his enemies. The young playwright, who has been exasperating him by refusing to do rewrites demanded by the director, has just asked the Old Producer how he liked working with Peter Brook.

OLD PRODUCER: How did I like working with Peter Brook? How did I like working with Peter Brook? You sit there, in all the arrogance of your fucking youth, about to throw a way the greatest and quite possibly the only such opportunity in your entire fucking lifetime, and all you can say is how did I like working with Peter Brook? You'd give it up so easily, after everything we've been through, everything we've worked for, all the fucking humiliations I've put myself through to help you, calling up this person and begging that person and staking my fucking reputation on this Goddamned play, everything I've been through to help you, because I believe in you, I believe this is damned good writing, better than 90 percent of the crap I got rich producing, and all you can think about is how I liked working with Peter Brook? Who gives a good flying shit about Peter fucking Brook?

What do you think this is about, anyway? Do you think this is about money? Do you think I've spent my whole fucking life doing this because I wanted to get rich? I can get rich any fucking time I please. I've gotten rich more times than I can remember and lost it and got it back again and lost it again. It's not the money I come for. It's the fight. I love the fight. To show those bastards. To show the bastards I can win. To beat those people. It's a war. Don't kid yourself. The theater's not a lot of artsy-fartsy pansy prancing around tap dancing hugs and kisses. The theater is war. It's war. Fought to the death. No rules. Just cunning and a relentless, ruthless willingness to cut the other guy's throat from ear to ear with a smile on your face, a shine on your shoes, and a fucking melody in your heart. It always has been. It always will be.

Cairo
Arthur Melville Pearson

Dramatic

James Jr. (late twenties)

> James Jr. believes that at midnight tonight, his long-deceased mama and grandparents are coming to pick him up in a blue '51 Chevy. His father and sisters have gathered in his converted chicken coop house on the family farm in Cairo (pronounced KAY-ro), Illinois, to see him through this latest apparent schizophrenic episode spurred by the imminent sale of the farm. But near the end of the play, placing a handful of soil in each of his family members' hands, his wild talk interlaced with snippets of beloved poems sets everyone to thinking that he might not be so crazy after all.

JAMES JR.: It's no secret, but seems like seldom we remember that this dirt is why we're here. We put blade to soil, sow our seeds within the bones and hopes of those who've come before us and those who've left too soon, and most of the time we scan our fields and see nothing but tasseled waves of green, but comes a time, every once in a while, we look out across our land and our eye falls upon an area of stunted growth, and we suspect the yield will be less than we had hoped, if anything at all. Was it draught, acid soil, rootworm or tipworm, or was it just bad seed? We can't help but spring from those who sowed us and as we all return from whence we sprang, there's nothing really to be forgiven, but do we tend the disappointing patch with any less love than the surrounding stalks, or just plow it under and make like we forget? For the answer, we need just weigh this dirt against our heart. Sing Rum tiddy um/tiddy um/tiddy um tum tum and offer up, "Oh, my heart which I had from my mother, do not rise up against me as a witness in the presence of this Earth, do not speak against me for what I have failed to remember, I remember that I am not a separate thing from the Earth, I remember that the Earth keeps some vibration in your heart and that is you and I remember that flowers grow in me even as I walk the fields, woodlands, and prairies of my native state. I am this Earth, waiting for all good friends to remember that Out of me unworthy and unknown/The vibrations of deathless music/"With malice toward none, with charity for all"/Out of me the forgiveness of millions toward millions. Sing Rum tiddy um/tiddy um/tiddy um tum tum and Good friends, let's to the fields, I have a fever . . . and, well . . . you remember the rest, don't you?

Chain Mail
Frederick Stroppel

Seriocomic

Nicky (twenties to thirties)

Nicky is becoming increasingly paranoid, and here he is ranting to his wife/girlfriend, Danielle.

NICKY: Don't you know what's going on? Don't you know what terrible things are happening out there?

In the world! The world is teeming with horrors! Nightmares! Plagues real and metaphorical! People being killed, persecuted, enslaved — enduring sufferings and deprivations of body and soul on a scale we can scarcely fathom. Why them? Why not *me?* Why should *I* be spared? Because I'm *special?* No, I always knew this day was coming; it was only a matter of time. Sooner or later they had to find me, zero in, trial and error, process of elimination . . . And now it's here, right here! This letter with no return address, no distinguishing features, nothing about it but an inescapable aura of doom — why was it sent to *me,* and why today? Because it's *my turn!* Does it make sense to be beaten to death, or raped by your parents, or tortured and mutilated by the friendly cop on the corner? No, but it's happening, isn't it, right in this city, right this very minute! You could be walking down the street right now, whistling your happy tune, enveloped in your cozy cocoon of ignorance, and then suddenly you're face down on the sidewalk, drowning in your own blood, cut down by a bullet or a box-cutter or a runaway cab or an exploding gas main . . . Anything! For no reason! Is there sense in that? Is that logical? *(Beat.)* I never told you this, Danielle . . . About a month ago I was taking the subway home. And when I got off at Astor Place I was stopped by a man who said he was a detective. He showed me a photo of a little girl, said she was missing, wondered if I'd seen her. And I said no, I hadn't, which was true. Then he asked me my name and address. *My* name, *my* address. Why? I knew nothing about the case; why would he need to get in touch with me?

Circumference of a Squirrel

John Walch

Dramatic

Chester (twenty-eight)

> Upon his father's death, Chester is left with emptiness and contemplates the bond that holds him to his father.

CHESTER: *(Gets Lifesaver from his pocket.)* Lifesavers. My father always carried a roll of wint-o-green Lifesavers in his pocket. He doled them out as largess for small tasks done: taking out the trash, getting wood for the fire, helping clear the dishes . . . and . . . occasionally just for no reason at all. Sometimes I'd fake being sick, act like I had a *cough,* just waiting for Dad to notice: *"You need a Lifesaver, Chetie?"* When I was in college, he never once sent me a letter, but every once in awhile, I would get this brown, bubble-wrapped envelope in the mail that said: FRAGILE in big red letters on the outside. FRAGILE. And inside, wrapped to an inch of its life in toilet paper, was a roll of wint-o-green Lifesavers. No note, no check, nothing — just a roll of wint-o-green Lifesavers. *(Holding out Lifesaver to audience.)* FRAGILE. *(To himself.)* Fragile. *(Shift.)* His eyes are wide open, pupils the size of two silver dollars. I stand over the hospital bed studying those pupils for a sign. Maybe, maybe if I look straight into them, straight into his eyes I will discover the mystery that will allow me to weep. *(Pause.)* But his eyes, those silver dollars, offer me nothing — nothing but a reflection of myself. My mother slumps in a corner chair. She sobs in fits and starts. My brother puts away the board games. But he puts Risk pieces in with the Monopoly set and mixes the pegs of Mastermind in with the Battleship set. As he stacks the boxes on the windowsill, he slams them together. A nurse stands patiently by the door. On the bedside table, sits a roll of wint-o-green Lifesavers — one left. "Fragile." I hold it, hoping to be saved. Hoping for something. But there's nothing. I am twenty-eight years old. My father has just died and I feel nothing. Neither pleasure or pain — nothing.

Creatures Lurking in the Churchyard
Don Nigro

Dramatic

John Ruffing (thirty-six)

> John Ruffing, an English police inspector, very good at what he does, age thirty-six, sits in a chair in his study in London in the year 1901. On a small table before him is a revolver. He is deciding whether to kill himself. His young wife, whom he loved desperately, has just died under mysterious and terrible circumstances, and Ruffing, a person whose life has been devoted to the solving of puzzles made of other people's tragedy, has found himself plunged into despair so deep he doesn't believe he can continue. His own despair is a puzzle he can't seem to solve except by ending his life. But there is the problem of what will become of his daughter.

JOHN: Getting the ending right is the worst thing.

And so no one returns to the matter of suicide. To the matter of ending one's pain, of making a terrible mess in the study, amid the ticking of the clocks, amid the ticking of the clocks.

There is no proper way to communicate this. For a person in the midst of this particular unending hell cannot make a person not in it understand his hell. A person who is not in hell merely believes himself not to be, is in a state of denial, of temporary illusion. Soon enough the scales will fall from his eyes, and when they do, he will look around and see the true landscape of hell, which has been there all along, and he also will not be able to properly communicate the nature of his hell to others. Monads have no windows. It is all looking into dark mirrors.

Structure is always the most difficult thing. I have spent my life solving puzzles, and repairing ancient clockworks. I have loved perhaps too deeply. It is not advisable to love too deeply. It only encourages the demons. And now I come to the end, here in this room, with a ticking clock and a revolver, and I find that I —

Do not think for a moment that there is anything after. No, I do not think there is. But what if it is this? Or what if I am already dead, and this is my own particular hell, and is thus forever. What if one should put the gun to one's head, and pull the trigger, and discover that nothing has changed, that one's own particular afterlife is to suffer forever the anguish which caused one to end the play of one's life?

Or if the end, if all ends, then why imagine the daughter will suffer? Do you see? For if ending my brain ends the universe, there will be no daughter to suffer, as the end of my suffering will mean also the end of her, the end of London, the end of Afghanistan, the end of all creatures. But I do not believe that. Because I can imagine the world going on without me, without my knowledge of it. Them finding me here in the study, my brains splattered against the wall. She will see it in her head. She will see it forever in her head.

So what is the conclusion to the matter? Life is suffering. Suffering is caused by desire. Eliminate desire and you eliminate suffering. How does one eliminate desire? Follow the eightfold path. What is the eightfold path? A labyrinth in which one becomes lost. There is no answer. There is only hell. Hell is everything and hell is forever. One must simply suffer. Suffering is all. It is all made of agony.

A ticking clock. Night in the old house. In the churchyard, little rustlings in the leaves. Red eyes of the damned.

(The light fades on him. Just the ticking in darkness.)

Doctor Faustus
Don Nigro

Dramatic

Faustus (about forty)

> Dr. John Faustus, about forty, fabled sixteenth-century physician and would-be sorcerer, bored with his life and horrified at the plague-ravaged world he sees around him, has summoned up the Devil, who turns out to be a beautiful but enigmatic young woman, with whom he has become increasingly obsessed. By the terms of their bargain for his soul, he can have anything that's in her power to give him, including her flesh, but love is forbidden. She frustrates him because he can't understand her, can't figure out whether she really cares for him or not. He has just demanded that she tell him what she really thinks of him, and her reply, that he is in fact a cold, selfish, insecure, terrified, and desperate person, has so unnerved him that he has struck her violently across the face, knocking her to the ground. He looks down at her, horrified at what he's done, and speaks.

FAUSTUS: I told you to shut up. You're supposed to obey me. Did that hurt? Oh, come on. Devils do not feel pain. You've told me as much yourself. This is all just a game to you. We're just finding new games to play, that's all. You didn't feel a thing. The Devil doesn't feel a thing, does she? What's that awful noise you're making? Is the Devil sniffling? Is she? Is the Devil crying? Ohhh, poor Devil. I dislike that intensely. It bores me. I find that most unpleasant. If you keep that up, I most certainly will slit your throat. Hell, I might slit MY throat. My God, what a disaster I am. You're very good at that, Devil. Quite realistic. I may cry myself. Could you teach me how? Do you know, when I began this thing, I didn't even believe in you. Did you know that? I think one who believes in you belongs to you already. Is that true? Devil? Oh, hell. Poor Devil. There's no hope at all for you, is there? Me neither. What hope is there for a man who can make the Devil cry? I'm afraid you're my damnation, and I'm yours. Is that how it works? Is it? God help me. God help us both. Now we're in for it. Yes we are. Consummatum est.

The Faculty Room
Bridget Carpenter

Dramatic

Carver (twenties to thirties)

Carver, a high school teacher, has recently been hired at this school. He is rather fresh-faced and naïve, and is having difficulty dealing with the cynicism and game playing of the other teachers. They finally goad him into revealing why he left his last teaching job.

CARVER: *Love* him?! Love Sam? He was an *annoyance*. He jeopardized my — everything. He fucked up my career.

I wanted to do good things, really good things. My first classroom. Then: the letters. The unceasing letters. Messages on chalkboards. All about me. I had to erase the board at the beginning of every class, every day. I called his parents. I filed a report with the district. The response? I should be able to *handle* a "crush."

So. I met with Sam. He brought me roses.

I told him his behavior was inappropriate. I said he was in danger of being expelled. Sam said fine, great, perfect: Then we could be together. He tried to kiss me. He said we were "soul mates." And something rose up in me. And I said:

"Sam. This all has to stop.

I don't love you.

I don't *like* you.

You don't matter to me. You don't matter."

And Sam — backed away. He said "OK." He walked out and I breathed a sigh of relief. I did it! I would have my classroom back. I would have my life back. Later that night, he bought gasoline and . . . you know the rest.

I wasn't afraid to love him. I really didn't. Love him. I was his teacher, and I showed exactly how much I cared. Not at all.

Eight Days (Backwards)
Jeremy Dobrish

Dramatic

Mr. Goldberg (thirties to forties)

> Goldberg, a high-powered executive, is having regular sex with a maid named Consuela, to whom he speaks here.

MR. GOLDBERG: I know it's a little early in the day for the bubbly, but a promotion's a promotion. And right now I'd much rather get drunk and climb on top of you than call Sheila and get belittled and berated. Bottoms up.

You think I'm not a good husband am I right? Because of the things I say. Well I am a good husband. Hell, I took Sheila to the airport on Saturday myself Goddamn it. No fucking car service. Took her right to the gate, sixteen hundred and four bucks for a first-class ticket straight down the toilet. And that's devotion whether she sees it or not. And I'm certainly a hell of a lot better than your deadbeat husband who left you. You probably . . . , what?, met him, and he would do anything to win you over, and you thought he was someone special. Someone better than you. Well where is he now? A good man does not leave his family. A good man keeps his family together and that is what I do and I am a good man. And a good husband. I do what I have to do to keep my marriage together. Period. And you want to know something, Consuela? Having sex with you is when I feel the most alive. The most . . . powerful. Really. I mean that as a compliment. I mean, if you don't enjoy fucking, then what the hell is there? What's left? I need you. I do. Without you, life would be . . . just . . . grey. *(He reaches into his pants pocket and removes his wallet. He takes out two hundred dollar bills.)* Look at me, Consuela. I know you're not a prostitute. And you know you're not a prostitute. But me leaving extra money in your envelope each time we . . . it's just silly. We both know what we're doing. We have a mutually beneficial . . . business arrangement. Take it. Just take it. Oh for God's sake take it. I know you need it.

Eight Days (Backwards)
Jeremy Dobrish

Dramatic

Jonathan (early twenties)

> While trying to pick up a woman named Selena in a bar, Jonathan goes on and on about his unhappy life.

JONATHAN: OK. Hi, I'm Jonathan Kaplan. I graduated from Yale two years ago with a degree in English lit aka "You want fries with that." That's a joke. Sorry. My father is an analyst. Not of people but of numbers. Don't ask, I don't know what it means either. My mother's a Jewish Mother. Nuff said. Despite the statistics, they're still happily married. I grew up on Long Island and am very happy to be living in the City though I wish I had more money because then I fantasize that I might actually enjoy myself. On the other hand, I desperately want to live in the country because then I fantasize I might actually enjoy myself. I spend a disproportionate amount of time convincing myself that I can live both in the City and in the country at the same time. When not actively engaged in self-delusion, I spend my time writing a novel but then, who doesn't? Or at least who didn't until writing the great American software code took over for writing the great American novel. I'm not terribly athletic but I religiously read the sports page and get angrier when the Knicks miss a foul shot than I do when the U.S. bombs a foreign country. I have an older brother, Marty, who went to MIT, partnered up with some friends in Seattle on "Here's something you don't need"-dot-com and made a buzzillion dollars. Then lost a buzzillion dollars. He has stopped returning my phone calls. I have a younger sister, Jessica, who insists that everyone call her Selena because she feels the pain of the murdered Latin American rock star, and who just dropped out of school for the second time. This time to follow her forty-five year-old ex-hippie boyfriend on a trek through the Himalayas. She doesn't believe in phones despite the obvious evidence to the contrary. I imagine that one day I'll recount this time in my life to my wife or my kid or my mistress I suppose if things go terribly wrong, and I'll reminisce about how great it was and how happy I felt, but right now, I gotta tell you, it feels like crap. I definitely aspire to greatness but eagerly accept mediocrity. I try to think globally and act locally, but mostly I just eat a lot of Haagen-Dazs, and I realize that there is no "I" in team, but basically don't care. I prefer autumn to spring, feel stupid in shorts, and look forward to one day actually needing a suit for something other than a funeral or wedding. I consider myself a "cautious realist" while most people consider me a raging pessimist. And although I don't believe in God, and have nothing resembling faith in the spiritual, yesterday I went to a fucking palm reader because if I don't make some human contact soon, I'm going to shoot myself. Now then, I have about seven minutes, why the fuck are you in such a bad mood?

The Fourth Wall
A.R. Gurney

Comic

Floyd (forties to fifties)

> Floyd, a college theater professor, understands Peggy's point in designing her abode as if it were a stage set.

FLOYD: What you're saying is that any culture which cannot produce good theater, and a good, solid audience to respond to it, is no culture at all. What you're also saying — now don't let me put words in your mouth — but what you might be saying is that most great nations — be it Greece in the age of Pericles or Elizabethan England — have produced great theater when they were at their peak. And maybe you're saying as well that we ourselves have had a whiff of that greatness even in this country, in the period from Eugene O'Neill through Arthur Miller, when indeed our country was hitting its stride as a world power. And you're also saying that now that our theater has declined, you're concerned that our greatness as a nation is declining as well. And therefore, this wall, and your yearning to reach beyond it, is an attempt to revitalize theater in America and to keep our great country from sliding irrevocably into philistinism and decay. God, Peggy! You don't know how exciting this is! This afternoon, I was sitting alone in my office, hoping that one of my students in American Drama might stop by at least to chat. I knew this was unlikely, however, because this semester I am down to three students in that course: an ambitious young man who wants to write film scripts, a breathless young woman who saw *Les Miz* in fourth grade, and an exchange student from Bangladesh who signed up by mistake. Normally I would have used my spare time to prepare for next semester's course on World Drama, but I learned today that it's just been supplanted by a second section of a new course in Media Studies entitled The Brady Bunch and Beyond.

The General from America
Richard Nelson

Dramatic

Washington (midforties)

> General Washington is here bellyaching to one of his trusted generals about perfidy in Congress. His confidant? Gen. Benedict Arnold.

WASHINGTON: Well, we're not here to talk about me. Mr. Adams has proposed in Congress that all generals should be elected. I wrote and said, great. I vote for Mr. Adams to be on the front lines. *(Beat.)* He withdrew his proposal. They don't know what they are doing. And they're bringing us all down with them. Tell me, what is the currency rate on the street? No one will tell me.
  (Beat. Pause.)
  I tell them, get someone else. I'm not a military genius. Get Gates. He wants it bad. Look what he did to Schuyler. Just because the man disagreed with him. No one wants to discuss anything anymore. Everyone's screaming at everyone. Who's the real American? And they're all just such Goddamn hypocrites! Your Mr. Reed, your accuser — he's trying to bring God into this now. What the hell does God have to do with a war? If he'd been with us this winter — he'd have had to conclude that if he wanted to be on God's side, it wasn't ours. *(Short pause.)* There was a moment last winter — Hamilton knocked on my cabin. Twenty men — enlisted — wanted to see me. More desertion. More failure. They come in. I just look into the fire, waiting for them to begin to justify — their families. Their farms. They're hungry. Who gives a shit, they're soldiers! But . . . . *(He shrugs.)* Then, one begins to speak, a young boy really — how they have come to enlist again — for another year. In the midst of a blizzard. They had no shoes, Benedict. I looked at them. In the firelight.

Their eyes red from sickness. Their clothes torn and bloody. And I went to each one . . . . *(He begins to cry.)* And I hugged them. I held them. I told them how proud of them I . . . . (*Washington wipes the tears, pours himself a glass of rum.*) Rum. What did I tell you? *(He drinks.)* Are you broke too?

(Short pause.)

Sometimes you feel like an utter fool. Everyone's getting rich. Everyone I know it seems. Is that what this was really about — money? *(Beat.)* Makes you want to curse — the whole species, Mr. Arnold. It can't just be an American trait, Benedict. It must be everyone. Somehow that gives some comfort.

The General from America
Richard Nelson

Dramatic

Sir Henry (fifties)

> Sir Henry, a British general during the American revolution, is here
> talking to the traitor Benedict Arnold pleading with him to help save
> Major Andre, who has been arrested by the Continental army as a
> spy and is to be hung.

SIR HENRY: *(Shouts.)* Think about it, I said! And you'd better do just that,
because I am the only hope you have now — you have no country,
no home, no friends, no family; all you've got is me! *(Pause.)* No-
bility, by the way, cannot be discussed in "pragmatic terms." At least
I wouldn't know how. But perhaps you people have never understood
that. You are so crude. Sir, this may be America, but in this office at
least it is still the king's country and here the world is not only about
business and money. There is something greater. Something you in
this godforsaken piece of Earth can't seem to understand! A decency!
Virtue! And yes, honor! *(Beat.)* In my two years here, sir, I have
searched with great interest to discover what you Americans in fact
believe in. Besides of course the freedom to cheat each other. I look
in vain. Yours is a hollow race. Which, with each day — each new
dawn, each new . . . *(He nods to Arnold.)* acquaintance, only disgusts
me more. *(Short pause.)* He is a beautiful man. Andre. Like a god.
A good *English* lad — worth, one would think, slightly more than
a horde of your kind. That's my personal belief. My moral belief.
(Beat.) For what it's worth. *(He smiles to Arnold.)* What do you have
to live for, General Arnold? You've failed even us. You're despised —
even by us. You think my soldiers will have anything but contempt
for someone like you? *(He gestures to him.)* What is there to respect?

So what is left? Sooner or later, you too will come to this conclusion. Why not sooner — and to save a life? *(Short pause.)* The rebels have agreed to allow your wife — Peggy? — to join you here. *(Beat.)* She has refused. *(He hands Arnold Peggy's letter.)* She's chosen, she writes, to return to her family in Philadelphia, where she intends to seek an annulment of her marriage to the greatest scoundrel her young country has ever known. I don't think she's joking. *(Arnold looks at the letter.)* She hates you . . . The list grows and grows. Trade yourself, damn it! Die with dignity, not in some back room! Save a good man!

God of Vengeance

Donald Margulies

Adapted from a play by Sholem Asch,
based on a literal translation by Joachim Neugroschel

Dramatic

Jack (thirties)

> Jack is a fairly recent Jewish immigrant to America. Here, he prays
> to God.

JACK: *(Whispers to the scroll.)* Hello, God. It's me, Yankel Tshaptshovitsh.
Welcome to my home. God, you see everything. You know everything I do. If you want to punish me, punish me. But the innocent
girl who sleeps here — this angel — doesn't know the meaning of
the word sin. Have pity on her. Amen. *(Sits, whispers gently to the
form lying in bed.)* Rivkele? I don't want to wake you. I just want to
be near you. *(He pulls up a chair and sits.)* I used to sit by your cra-
dle while you slept, just to listen to you breathe. I couldn't believe
the perfect little miracle God gave to two sinners! You are not the
work of a vengeful God, my darling. *(A beat.)* I had to find my way
by myself, on the street. A greenhorn in America, a scrawny orphan.
What did I have? I had nobody; I had nothing. Just my wits. But
you, my precious, you're gonna have the life in America we only
dreamed about. You, and your children. Yankel's children. You'll live
the dream. *(A beat. More hurt than anger.)* So, when I find out you've
been going downstairs when I told you never to go downstairs . . .
When I find out you're making friends with the wrong sort of people . . . And lying to me! Sweetheart! Is it any wonder I get upset?
I'm better now. I had a talk with your mother. I've calmed down.
We'll talk in the morning. Everything will be all right. *(He reaches
for "her" and is shocked to find pillows where he thought she lay. He
flings off the blanket and shouts in horror.)* Oh my God! NO!!!!!

Gogol
Don Nigro

Seriocomic

Gogol (forties)

Gogol, the great Russian writer, in his forties, looking much older, wild hair, wild eyes, long nose, wearing an overcoat in his murky bedroom in 1852. He is in the process of losing his mind while the Drowned maiden in his bed cuddles in the lap of a giant nose he has been chasing around the room. He remembers his first sexual experiences and attempts to understand how art has been for him an unsuccessful substitute for intimacy, preparatory to burning his masterpiece and starving himself to death.

GOGOL: As a young man I once went with some friends to a brothel, but I didn't enjoy it very much. Several times in fact I failed to enjoy it. I enjoyed it so little that I kept doing it again and again in the hope that somehow I could discover what was such a big deal about it. Finally the poor girl was exhausted so I went home and ate sausages. *(He sits down on the bed with them.)* At first, you see, and perhaps for many years, in fact, creation, that is, writing, which is to say, fantasy, or perhaps rather barefaced lying to one's self, is a kind of substitute for love, and perhaps this works for some time, perhaps not very well, perhaps not so well as to make one happy, exactly, or even close to that, or even to prevent one from being very miserable, but at least it works perhaps for a while at least well enough to keep one from putting a revolver into one's mouth, say, and blowing one's brains out the back of one's head and splattering them all over the rose pattern wallpaper. But after a time, you see, after a time, creation, that is, writing, that is, hallucination, becomes less and less an adequate substitute for love, for physical contact, for emotional intimacy, until, you see, until one is filled with such emptiness, such unspeakable loneliness and such profoundly humiliating misery that one begins, finally, not to create any longer, but rather to destroy, and in particular to destroy what one has previously created, as God, for example, is wont to do, but the truth is that destruction does not really satisfy, either, until all that remains to one, finally, is to destroy one's self, which, if one has not the courage to insert the barrel of the gun carefully into one's mouth and gently but firmly squeeze the trigger, leaves one with only the nose left dripping in the cabbage soup, with grease on one's cheeks and a black hole in one's heart, and thus the only option left to one, said the nose, is to simply refuse to eat, which is what, in the end, I have done, and I believe this is the end, you'll be happy to know, and thus a determined self-starvation is exactly what I have been doing these past few weeks, here on this particular carousel, here among the mad faces of all the cannibal carousel horses, and this willful renunciation of all nourishment has, remarkably, been productive of some of my very best hallucinations. *(He finds a fat manuscript.)* Ah. Here's what I've been looking for. This should burn very nicely. *(He puts the manuscript in the fire.)* Yes. This is burning wonderfully. It's the Second Part of *Dead Souls,* which I've been working at for ten years. It's all right. It's merely the only copy of the summit of my life's work, which is to say, of course, that it's absolute rubbish.

Gogol
Don Nigro

Seriocomic

Gogol (forties)

The great, Russian writer, Gogol, in his forties but looking much older, wild hair, wild eyes, long nose, wearing an overcoat, sitting in his murky bedroom in 1852. He is in the process of losing his mind, having a possibly imaginary conversation with a Drowned Maiden he has found in his bed, and two hand puppets, the Devil and the Gypsy Girl, one on each hand. He has serious issues with women, who both obsess and horrify him, and his work, which he obsessively creates and then burns, and his increasing frenzy here is evidence that he has just about reached the end of his rope, his sanity, and his life.

GOGOL: No. No more touching. There will be no more touch. Touching is nothing but agony. Agony. Why must you torment me so? I am not the man who slept with Pushkin's wife. I never shot Pushkin in the glockenspiel. I know who you are. You are one of those Chinese soul-stealers. I saw you swimming naked at Reichenbach Falls. I got drunk with you once in a Munich hotel room. Well, no more of that. No other swamp creates more violent fevers than the bog of Melancholia, and I am the parings of God's holy toenails. There shall be no more touch now forever. Be quiet, all of you. I think I'm having a vision. Yes. Catherine the Great is sleeping with her horse. He is feeling his oats. She is also feeling his oats. Now the vampire girl is copulating with the writer in the hayloft while the barn is burning. She is above, he below. He holds her two breasts in his hands. At the moment of climax she bites deep into his neck, and his hot red blood spurts all over her face and breasts. In the old stone house, everybody has a stomachache, and the housemaids are continually becoming pregnant. The little gray cat goes off into the woods and is repeatedly violated by screaming wild tomcats. The old woman can hear their love songs from her cold bed. *(He makes the hideous sounds of mating cats.)* Yeooorrrrllllllll. Yeoorrowoworowlllllllllll. The return of a missing cat is always a portent of death. Also a woman who bites off your ear is a sign of bad luck. In my dreams I am screwing a goose. *(He makes a loud honking noises of goose passion and outrage.)* Honka honka honka honka honka! Honka honka! Honka! There is also the hideous face of a pig at the window. *(He makes threatening pig sounds.)* Snork snork snork snork snork snork! Draw a face, win a pig! I would shoot this pig, but my weapon has become rusty from disuse. The neck of the goose. The snout of the pig in the courthouse. I dream of the wet breasts of the lovesick bell ringer. And the rain falls all day and all night. Oh, it's a dreary world, ladies and gentlemen. Taras Bulba. Taras Bulba. I am the ruler of the gnomes, you know. My eyelids reach down to the ground. *(Howling like a wolf.)* AOOOOOOOOO. AOOOO. AOOOO. AOOOOOOOOO. The distant howling of a wolf. Full moon tonight.

The Golem

H. Leivick

Adapted by David Fishelson, from a translation by Joseph C. Landis

Dramatic

Thaddeus (thirty plus)

> Thaddeus, a priest in Prague, in the late sixteenth century, here ad-
> dresses a disparate group of townspeople and beggars.

THADDEUS: His kind can amputate a leg
    And keep it hidden in a bag
    And when they need it, take it out again.
    They live like kings up here as though they owned the place.
    The walls are filthy, full of nails;
    The air so foul it takes your breath away.
    To think that here once lived in glory
    Our gentlemen and nobles!
    That these louse-ridden floors
    Once felt the step of royal feet.
    Now all is ruin. *He* has been cast out,
    The tears that dripped in sorrow from His crown of thorns,
    Which they, grim unbelievers, stuck into His brow. *(To the beggars.)*
    Why do you gape and stand around?
    You live among us, angry and embittered,
    And wear your anger as he wears his hump.
    Haven't we tortured you enough,
    Oppressed you, burnt you, led you out to slaughter?
    We've grown weary of our hatred,
    Yet still you parade your zealotry before us
    And clench your teeth in obstinate tenacity —
    And all the more, you smash our dreams of peace,
    And all the more, you stoke in us the fires of hate.
    No peace can ever be between us —

You haunt us like an evil dream.
We cannot share one Earth with you,
Warmed by the same sun, breathing the same air.
The air your lungs inhale becomes noxious to our hearts;
And our hearts yearn for *peace and calm,*
For respite and release from you.
You sit upon our conscience and our brain
Like black spiders in a knot . . .
You say that we accuse you falsely,
And you scurry and you work to prove us liars.
You defend yourselves —
Why do you lack the courage to proclaim it
To the world, with dignity and pride,
And say: Yes, we do drink blood for Passover!
It's what binds our unleavened bread!
We've always drunk it, always will! *(Laughs at his own words.)*
We burn you at the stake, and though you're innocent,
You go as willingly to be burned as if invited to a ball!
Why don't you attack us
As we do you, with torch and axe?
And even now, this moment, as I speak,
Why don't you answer?
Where is there one among you with the courage
To step forward, seize my staff,
And break it on my skull. You say nothing!
All you do is wait for me to shout: Get out!
Always, always ready to depart —
So be it, then, go! GO! *GET OUT!*

Good Boys
Jane Martin

Dramatic

Ethan (teens)

Ethan is a deeply disturbed teenager with a gun.

Ethan takes aim and fires his pistol three times from a double-handed firing position.

ETHAN: *(To the audience, after firing.)* Hey, I could make bucks. Stupendous bucks, man. I got the deal, dude, E-business and beyond. I am so serioso. "The Shooter's Guide to Millennial Parenting," right? "How to Disarm Little Jimmy and Johnny Right at Home in Your McMansion!" Let's apply our logic, logic, logic, shall we? Parents . . . troubled parents . . . here's the spike: From me you want grades, S.A.T.s, manners, submission to command, fiscal responsibility, cleanliness, whereabouts, and hey, listen up, *I don't care.* From you, I want enthusiasm for my creepy music, infantile anarchic politics, liberality toward my tasteless, filthy clothes, compliments for my piercings, uncomplaining launderings for my masturbations, but mainly . . . mainly, I want you to use your power on my behalf. Most particularly when I don't deserve it. I want you to dismay my enemies, trumpet my virtues always . . . always! I want to be your central concern, your constant thought, your wife, your husband, your job, your reason for being, because, hey, if not, holy moly, why did you have children, dude? But if you fail me . . . oh, if you fail me . . . hey, read your Shakespeare, stupid . . . I will take arms against a sea of troubles, and, by opposing, end them.

Good Boys
Jane Martin

Dramatic

Thomas (forties)

Thomas, a pastor, confronts the father of the boy who murdered his son.

THOMAS: I am a pastor, Mr. Erskine. A pastor who has fallen silent. I am not able . . . because . . . I am still so angry . . . so angry . . . excuse me . . . *(He walks away from James a step or two, controls himself, and turns back.)* . . . that I cannot stand before my congregation and preach the word of my God, and the word of my God is my personal salvation. I'm not playin' with you. As to "half-human," well you never met a man who could understand you better. Oh, I hear you. I am half-human when I cannot preach the word. So I see you and hear you clear. You understand me? We are in need of each other at this time. No, sir. I'm not some curiosity seeker, huh-uh. I'm not from the devil's press selling papers on sensation. *(James turns to go.)* One minute. You and I never met, Mr. Erskine, never in all the hearings or in all the trials, not in all the meetings or all those . . . I don't know what to call them . . . bloodsucking TV shows. I couldn't bear to be any part of it, James. Huh-uh. I couldn't bear to hear about it, couldn't bear to read about it . . . sent me off so my wife would lock herself in a room not to hear me. I would shut my ears and sit alone in silence, and then I would go to work at the warehouse so I could put bread on the table. I went back to church . . . my wife held my arm and walked me back there, but I couldn't preach in it, no way, no how, and I cannot do it to this hour. Cannot . . . do . . . it. *(A moment.)* Beg your pardon, but I see here you're drinkin' in the middle of the day. I know something about that. Oh, yes. I notice you cannot bear to hear about that day. There was a long time there . . . a long time . . . it made me physically sick to hear it, we are brothers on that score. We are prisoners in the puzzle of this thing, but I say to you every lock has a key. Every lock. So I came looking for you.

Hannah and Martin
Kate Fodor

Dramatic

Martin Heidegger (late fifties)

> *Hannah and Martin* is based on the lives of the Jewish political the-
> orist Hannah Arendt and her lover and mentor Martin Heidegger,
> the brilliant and charismatic German philosopher who was a vocal
> supporter of Hitler during World War II and never publicly apolo-
> gized for it. Hannah, who fled Germany to escape persecution, has
> returned on business after the war and is visiting the home that Mar-
> tin shares with his wife. Martin has been suspended from his teach-
> ing post at the university by the Allies and shunned by his former
> colleagues. He is in his late fifties but seems older because his health
> is suffering. Hannah and Martin are near the end of a long argu-
> ment in which she has demanded answers about his Nazism. It seems
> impossible that any friendship between them can be salvaged.

MARTIN: I was wrong, I was wrong, I was wrong to give Hitler my support. And I will apologize to the world when Hitler comes back to
apologize to me!

I had such hope — and here we are back in the same dull, petty,
filth-infested world we started out in. The same shit culture I was
trapped in before! And who will apologize to me?

These masses — these people whose opinions you are so anx-
ious that we shouldn't miss — have you spent any time with them?
They're money-grubbing and ignorant and loud. I've seen you move
away from such people on the train and yet you say you'd put your
future in their hands! Why is it wrong to say that they ought to take
their faces out of the funny papers and the ledgers of their fish shops
and read books and hear music and try to be of service to their fellow men? And what did I ever ask of my students and the others
around me except that?

I wanted to set us all free. I wanted us free from money and machines and our daily rounds of nothingness. I wanted us brave and brimming over with passion. I wanted a world where people were rewarded for having something other than water in their veins and chitchat on their lips. I wanted the world awake! Isn't that what you wanted, too?

An Infinite Ache
David Schulner

Seriocomic

Charles (twenties)

> Charles is working up the courage to propose to his girlfriend, Hope.

CHARLES: I've been thinking very hard about myself and my life and you which I didn't think I'd have to do at this stage in my life except I am so there it is but the thing about marriage is that I don't even know what the hell it is. I don't think anybody does until they do it and get divorced and try again, right? Then they'll know what to do. What mistakes there are to make, how to avoid them. So I mean I think wouldn't it be great if I could marry someone I didn't actually love for practice — I mean I know that's — but then I'll be ready to marry you with — after I get a divorce from — so our marriage has a better chance to make it. So forever won't be just another word. And love? Love?! I would rather . . . go swimming, you know? I hate that word. Love. It's so used up there's nothing left for me. For us. I'm just an ordinary guy but no one tells us how ordinary people should love. There's nothing I can feel that some woman in some fucking Jane Austen movie hasn't felt much stronger. Have you noticed that when people fall in love in movies you never hear what they're saying? And isn't that what really matters!? It always happens during some montage sequence when they're walking through a park or talking in the rain in a park, or having a picnic in the park — while it's raining. Something quirky and sexy because only quirky and sexy people deserve to fall in love. I mean what movie ever really captured a real, down-to-earth, boring, basic kind of love — OK maybe *Last Tango in Paris* but I don't see what good that does us in the end and I'm pretty sure I don't want you to stick your fingers up my ass. *(Beat.)* OK, by the look on your face it's clear you haven't seen that movie so let's um — the fingers you know, forget — if I wrote a movie everyone would get divorced and the movie would end. Because there's nothing I can say that would match the lift you get when you read Auden or Shakespeare. Oh, Shakespeare! Fuck him! He ruined everything! What's left for me? What can I give you that hasn't been given to someone else so much better? Do you even want that kind of love? Wouldn't you rather read about it? Or wait for the next movie? Love has fully evolved! Now it has to die like the dinosaurs before it can be reinvented. Since we've been living together I can feel us start to take each other for granted and while this should scream, "Warning! Warning!" it just doesn't matter! Um — I promised myself I wouldn't say "um." I just need to say that I can't promise anything. When we're up at the altar and the priest or the rabbi or the judge or whoever asks me, "Will you take Hope in sickness and in health: blah blah blah, I can't say, "I do." I just can't. Because how can you make a promise like that? How can you know? I can only say, "I will *try* my best," which I think means so much more in the long run, don't you? Hope? You know I can even say, "I will *promise* to try my best." And I know your parents will freak out and my father will never forgive me but I . . . I don't know anything — which is probably obvious now — I don't even know if I love you. I think I love you. I hope what I feel is love but I don't trust something that elusive and I don't think it's smart to plan your life around it. All I know is that now, at this moment — this brief little — that I want to spend my time with you — my life with you and only you. At least right now. So . . . I just want . . . to ask you . . . can we try to find love together — I mean the right — the question is — I mean traditionally — what I've been trying to — is — oh God, I didn't think this would be so — should I kneel or is that just — do I even have to ask — no, I'm going to ask since — so I think I've ruined the surprise by — OK here it comes — no that wasn't — OK, yes it was — Hope? Will you . . . will you . . . will you . . . *(Beat.)* Will you.

Laestrygonians
Don Nigro

Comic

McDuffy (midsixties)

Andrew McDuffy — an actor in his midsixties, leading man of a wonderful but always poverty-stricken English touring company in the year 1915 — is drinking with his fellow actors after a performance. He is a big, powerful, sardonic old Shakespearean, and although the years have begun to take their toll on him, he still loves his profession with a kind of fierce, ironic expression.

MCDUFFY: When you examine our life, you know, the entire basis of it is utter futility. We put the sets up, we tear the sets down, we do the show, we do the show again. Absolute futility. Creation, repetition, destruction, world without end, except that all worlds do end, as all created things die. We put on masks, we go in and out of doors, we pretend to love, to hate, to die, seek comfort, find disaster, play for laughs, play for tears, we play well, we play badly, moments of outrageous hope, moments of tremendous despair. Farce turns to tragedy and back again at the raising of an eyebrow. Hope is the killer. And only from despair does real power come. From darkness. We come out of the darkness and return to darkness. So dark in the house sometimes you don't know if there's a damned audience or not. Theater is the best and only metaphor because it is flesh and blood. That's how old Willy saw it. One great, wretched, grotesque, lovely, hideous Elizabethan-Jacobean blank verse rhymed couplet prose song and dance dumb show artificial head bouncing blood and thunder word burping monstrosity, monstrously beautiful, rather over written, but as intoxicating as sex with the innkeeper's daughter. *(He drinks.)* What's the matter, Mahoney? You've just turned white as the Queen's rump. Was it something I said? Come on. Don't be mysterious. Leave that to young John here. You know, Johnny, you bloody idiot, if you could play your own life half as well as you do Edgar, you'd be a happy man. And you play Edgar abominably. Ripeness. You must say the damned peee. Ripppeness. Do you think these bloody cretins have read the play? Only the intellectual cretins have read it, and they're too fucking smug to pay attention. They can only see what they've been taught to see. They're too busy following along with their fingers to notice me spewing my guts all over the stage. Ripppppppeness. Christ. I am doomed to squander my greatness before imbeciles. We're performing for livestock and persons who urinate off wagons.

Laestrygonians
Don Nigro

Dramatic

Mahoney (forty-seven)

> James Mahoney, a gifted and usually quite funny little Irish charac-
> ter actor in McDuffy's fabled but poverty-stricken Shakespearean
> touring company, Fool to McDuffy's Lear, is fond of asking people
> in bars what the worst thing they've ever done is. Here, age forty-
> seven, in the year 1924, he sits backstage after a performance, try-
> ing to convince his old friend John Rose to return to their dying
> company and help save it. He says if John will come back, he'll fi-
> nally tell what the worst thing he himself has ever done.

MAHONEY: The last time my father hit me, I stole money from the church
box and ran away in a terrible storm. It was like the Devil was after
me. I was soaked and exhausted when I came to an old farmhouse
in the middle of the night. I could see candles burning inside. I
banged on the door and was told to go away, but I made up some
story I was studying for the priesthood and lost my way in the storm,
and finally an old woman let me in. She was in much distress. Her
granddaughter had just died, and the old man was ailing as well, and
there was no priest nearby. She asked me to stand vigil and pray
over the dead girl's body while she tended her sick old husband. I
couldn't very well refuse. She led me up to the attic, and there was
the body of a girl, covered by a sheet. The old woman went downstairs and I sat there in the storm with the corpse of this young girl
and candles all around, pretending to pray, and I decided I wanted
to have a look at her. So I pulled the sheet down, just to her shoul-
ders. She was so beautiful. The old woman had just washed her, and
I felt this uncontrollable desire to see her naked body. So I pulled
the sheet off her. God, she was perfect. I had this desperate urge to
touch her. I touched her face. The body was still warm. I kissed her

lips, very tenderly and chastely, reverently. But the moment I did, I was consumed with lust, I'd never had a woman. I kissed her breasts, her stomach, her thighs. I thought I'd go mad with desire. Before I could properly think what I was doing I was making love to the creature. I know it sounds grotesque, but with the storm, and the candles, and the house at the end of the world, it seemed like a kind of eerie ritual, almost a holy thing, some sort of Druid resurrection ceremony. When it was done, I kissed her lips and pulled the sheet back up over her. I was weeping with shame but, God help me, I wanted her again. So I crawled out the window and jumped off the roof into a tree and back down into the rain. I left them the money I'd stolen from the church and ran and ran in the storm until I had no idea where I was. It was not long after I met up with McDuffy and he saw something in me, as he did with you. All these years, and still, when I make love to a woman, it's the poor dead girl I feel against my flesh.

The Late Henry Moss
Sam Shepard

Dramatic

Ray (thirties)

Ray and his brother Earl have inherited the hovel in which their father, recently deceased, spent his last days. Here Ray is talking to Earl about the old days, when they were a family, when he kept hoping Earl would stand up to the abusive old man.

RAY: Yeah. You remember how she used to scrub, day in and day out. Scrub, scrub, scrub.

You remember. You remember how she used to get everything spit-shined and polished — everything gleaming. The floors. The curtains. The tablecloth starched. All the glasses shining. You remember. Potatoes steaming on the plates. Carrots. Everything waiting. Everything perfect and just waiting like some kind of picture. You remember all that. And then — I used to think — I used to think she was doing all this work — all this preparation for us. And then, one day, it just — hit me. I don't know why. I just suddenly saw that it wasn't for us at all. It was for him. It was for Henry. Everything. All those hours and hours, slaving away — slaving away. It was for him. And then — And then, here he'd come! Bustin' in the door. You remember. "What the hell is everyone waitin' on me for? What're you waitin' on? The food's hot! Sit down and eat the food. Jesus H. Christ! You'd think this was some kinda Goddamn formal dinner here or something. You're hungry aren't ya? Sit down and eat!" *(Drops impersonation.)* And then everybody'd scramble to the table while he'd stomp the shit off his boots and throw his coat on the floor. You remember that? You remember how we'd all just sit there staring down into our napkins while he went on raving about the lack of rain or the price of citrus or the cost of feeding useless sons! Do you remember that, Earl! Do you remember that at all! You were there, Earl.

You were there the whole time. I remember your breath. The sound of your breath. Chopping away. I remember thinking, "He must be just as scared as me to be breathing like that. Just as full of terror!" But then I thought, "No, that's not possible. He's bigger than me. He's my big brother, How could he be scared?" And when she started screaming I thought Earl's gonna stand up for her. Earl's gonna take the weight. Earl's gonna stop him somehow! Because I knew, see. — I knew I didn't have a chance against him. I barely came up to his waist. All I could do is watch! And there she was — on the floor! Just like you, Earl. Just like you are now. Backed up under the sink! Crushed. He was kicking her, Earl! He was kicking her just like this! And every time he kicked her his rage grew a little bit and his face changed! His eyes bulged out and the blood rushed into his neck! And her blood was flying all over the kitchen, Earl! And still I kept thinking — I kept thinking — sooner or later Earl's gonna step in. Earl's gonna stop him. Earl's not going to let this happen, And just then — I looked out the kitchen window and I saw your car — your little white Chevy. Kicking up dust the whole length of the hay field. And that's the last time I saw you, Earl. That's the last time I saw you for a long, long while.

The Late Henry Moss
Sam Shepard

Dramatic

Ray (thirties)

> Ray and Earl, his brother, have inherited the hovel in which their recently deceased father spent his last days. They have been fighting over this house like a pair of dogs. Here, Ray has gotten the upper hand.

RAY: Get up off the floor! You know what I think? I think it's time we straightened up in here, don't you? Get a little order. I mean if I'm gonna be living here I'd like to have a little order. Scrub the floors maybe. The windows. Brighten the place up a bit. What do you think? How 'bout it, Esteban? You got a bucket around? A mop? No mop? No mop. How 'bout some rags, then? Must be some old rags around. Well, this will work. Now, here's what we're gonna do, Earl. This is my house now. So I want it clean. It's only natural. I want it spotless. I want it so you can eat right off the floor. So you can see the sun bounce off every little nook and cranny. Now, I want you to take this apron and get it wet. Get it wet now, Earl. Get it nice and wet and wring it out. Scrub every inch of this floor till it shines like new money! That's what I want you to do, Earl. I want you to do that for me, right now. Stuff really stinks bad, Esteban. Is it supposed to smell like that? Smells like something dead. This whole house stinks. Why is that? Is that from all your cooking, Esteban — over the years? Years and years of soups and chili and beans and shit? All that cooking. For what? What'd you think you were gonna do? Save Henry's puny life? Is that what you thought? Just keep scrubbing, Earl. We may have to disinfect this whole house. We may have to tear the walls down and rebuild the whole son of a bitch. Just to get the stink outta here. What is that stink? Can't you smell that? What smells like that? Maybe it's you, Earl. Is it you that smells like that? Esteban — Come over here and smell Earl. See what you think. Come on over here. *(To Esteban.)* Now, just bend down here and smell Earl. I can't tell anymore. I've lost track. What's he smell like to you? A man! Is that what a man smells like? *(Ray bends over and takes a long whiff of Earl, who keeps right on scrubbing through all this. Ray straightens up.)* Nah, I dunno — smells rotten to me.

Life in Refusal

Ari Roth

Dramatic

Ben (fifties)

> Ben is talking to a young woman named Alison about his experiences during World War II.

BEN: . . . So . . . I will tell you about 1943. Is quite interesting really, because I also have memory of meat pie. Actually, closer to potato pie, but all the same, texture is similar; this same taste of bread, wet blood, and tears. It is still middle of war, I am five, and we have just returned from Ural Mountains where my family is sleeping in basement of local library. On this very day of my return, young boy stops me on street and asks typical question of this time: "Who are you? Russian, or Jew?" And on answer "Jew," he hits me. "Socks me right in the kisser" is, I believe, the expression. I run to library, my face is swollen, all wet; and when I tell incident to my father, he has answered me in this way: "Benya," he tell me, "You can hit also." I can hit also. And so it began. For all my later life. I would fight any incident quite physically, I would fight it. And I would win. You know I am champion wrestler in high school? Also, swimming. Age 15. Freestyle. All the same, at this point, something changed. Less in me then in country. Around middle of 50s, acts of personal anti-Semitism became much less visible: much more clever. You see, when you are fighting against Man, you can see what you must hit. When you are fighting State, you are fighting endless chain. You cannot win or lose. State only allows or disallows, and always in arbitrary manner. In place of combat, spirit fights with self. And this is real genius of State: Elimination of Archetypal Enemy. All is "internal" now. Anti-Semitism exists only within imagination of each Jew. World watches in amusement as Jew eats self to death. Now again, act of brilliance: Refusenik as resister of Peace Train, putting ego and self-interest above "Good of Man," "Fight for Peace." I love peace. I can tell you. I would just like small piece of this peace for myself.

The Lucky Believe
David Cirone

Dramatic

Crayton (forties)

> After a tragic accident where his car strikes and kills a young boy,
> up-and-coming business executive Michael Ambrose wanders down-
> town in a state of shock and — on a whim — catches a Greyhound
> bus, abandoning the demands of his job and his marriage and trav-
> eling aimlessly around the country. He meets a high-energy stranger
> named Crayton, who involves him in a scam to steal money from
> rigged slot machines in Las Vegas. Michael follows through, but then
> decides to take the money home to the boy's family. Crayton tries
> to persuade him to stay for one more score.

CRAYTON: Look, really, truthfully here. Dig this — You know what I noticed, the first time I hit this city? Ain't changed, all these years —
Slot machines in the fucking airport! I'm talking before you take three
steps off the plane! You can't flush a fucking toilet in Vegas airport
without cha-ching, cha-ching, cha-ching . . . ! Fucking sucker slots.
The ones we've been playing — El Cortez, Lady Luck, Plaza, The
Royal — these are 95, 97 percent. OK, you wanna talk scam, this
is scam. These are the fucking true numbers, OK? This hotel we're
in, downstairs they got what — ? Hundred, hundred fifty of these
dollar slots? They're winning five bucks every five minutes off every
machine! Now the ones in the airport, we're talking state minimum
of 72 percent. They're not taking five bucks, they're taking twenty-
eight. Every five minutes. Now they lead you — they sucker you —
bright lights, big colors, lots of bells, that sound of money falling . . .
It's all about that five-year-old kid inside you that wants to put a
nickel in a machine and get some candy. So are they stealing? Is it
"thievery?" No. Of course not! It's "gambling," right? Just some harm-
less game, don't hurt anybody . . . Just kill your fucking mortgage

payment in the time it takes you to drop a few rum and cokes, right? *(Crayton downs the liquor in his glass.)* OK, listen — You know, I'm sorry about that thing I said before. I am. You told me that story about that boy, and I'm really very sorry. For you, for his family. That was a really shitty thing to go through. And your wife — she doesn't seem to be too easy to deal with, either. I mean — *(Laughs.)* I think you're a lot braver than I am, going back to her! You'll be lucky if she doesn't just shoot you! But — hey — that's your thing. I mean, marriage . . . doesn't it fucking kill you? My wife — she made these spinach and mushroom enchiladas once . . . I never came closer to my own mortality. *(Laughs, then —.)* OK . . . one of the men who runs this casino — this one, right here — I used to work for this man. And right now — *(Checks watch.)* — at two in the morning . . . my wife . . . is either fucking him or thinking about fucking him. Okay? And you're right — man, you are so right! — I don't care about his money! I'll take it all out to the desert and piss on it! But tomorrow — tomorrow I want this casino. And we can make it the last one. It can be the last one, and then everybody goes home. But this one, this one has to be in there. Because all of this . . . this money's his. It's his little candy for the month and he's gonna miss it. He's gonna miss it real bad. And I really, really need you for that. I need you. You understand me. *(Moves closer.)* You're the only one who gets it. The rules . . . don't . . . matter! The RULES don't MATTER! Human beings, the lines on the fucking road, the law, whatever — rules don't matter. Strength. Will. The will to do. The will to take. These men, the people on top — the people who are HAPPY — they all know it. You know it! You did it, just like me! You walked out. You walked over your line into freedom! So you're, you're, you're my proof! I know I'm right! Now, because of you, because of another human being, I'm right. Can't you see why that makes me happy? Isn't that what we all want to know? How the world works? What is the absolute TRUTH? Every choice we make is this "IF" — this "MAYBE" — Maybe if I do this, I'll be happy, maybe if I do this, she'll love me — maybe if I do this, my boss will give me a raise — maybe if I'm loyal, I'll be rewarded. So we play odds, right? How To Get What We Want. Money. Love. Happiness . . . But it's so easy. *(Pause.)* Take. *(Smiles.)*

Don't wait for love, take it. Don't wait for money. Take it. Don't wait for happiness. Take it. I mean, aren't you happy? Right now? *(Shoves some money against Michael's chest.)* Doesn't this make you happy? This money? *(Grabs more.)* Aren't you happy?

Man, Woman, Flower
Dan LaRocque

Comic

Jesse (twenties to thirties)

The play is set in a museum, suggested only by a large empty frame hanging downstage and two museum-style benches upstage of the "painting." Characters enter the room react to the downstage frame becoming a sketch of sorts themselves for the audience. In this monologue Jesse, a young, earnest, but over-stimulated, preacher reacts to the painting with a mixture of moral outrage and barely suppressed desire. While his rant confuses scripture with rock and roll, he does not sing. His lapses into popular music lyrics are delivered with the same reverence and in the same religious cadences he might employ from the pulpit in a particularly fiery sermon.

JESSE: *(Speaking to the unseen painting downstage.)* Smut and smut, I say again, nothing but smut! Lord have mercy upon us and smite the dirty demons, I look at this filthy painting and I say we must FIGHT, like knights in white satin, like riders on the storm, yea and verily even like a bad moon a rising, I say FIGHT for decency in art and respect! And yes, I know some might ask, "R-E-S-P-E-C-T? Why must ART have that for ME?" but we shall answer no longer with the sounds of silence! We, I say again, we have got to get out of this place. Where have all the Rockwells gone? Gone to Satan every one. When will they ever learn? When will they ever learn? How many roads must a man walk down, Christine, before we are free of such depravity? If I had a hammer, Christine, I'd hammer out this degenerate filth. I'd hammer in the morning; I'd hammer in the evening *(His wife tries to get him out of the room.)*. No Christine! Look, I say again look, at the disgusting, delicious, I mean malicious degradation that is unraveling the moral fabric of our society. This is the legacy of liberalism! Yes here's to YOU Mrs. Robinson! When art enters the gates of the soul, can depravity be far behind? It hurts, I say again, it really hurts so bad! This would not have happened in my father's day Christine, for yesterday all these troubles seemed so far away, but now we need a place to hide away. *(She again tries to pull him away from the painting.)* No Christine, no! We Will, We Will, ROCK them I say again, ROCK them out of this Gomorrah. Oh that I might be brought face-to-face with the lewd and luscious lady who modeled for this painting, that like a bridge over troubled water, I might lay me down and make straight her errant ways. For until that day I say I can't, I say again, I can't GET no satisfaction! The road is long, with many a winding turn, that leads who knows where, who knows where? It leads, I say again, it leads straight to hell by way of the satanic sixties, and depraved music of hippie flower people and already an evil lyric doth encroach upon my soul. For I am weary, feeling small, and friends just can't be found, yet I will prevail! I will ride forever 'neath the streets of Satan so that THIS *(Referring to the painting.)* might never return! *(He begins removing his coat and starts screaming at the painting.)* For you CAN'T, I say again, you can't always get what you want! I am the way, I am the *only* way! I am the truth! I am the *only* truth! I am a ROCK! I am an IIIIIIIsland! And a rock feels no pain! And an island never cries! *(He finally pulls himself together with some effort and then speaks with quiet certainty.)* After all, art isn't everyone's stairway to heaven!

Masha No Home
Lloyd Suh

Dramatic

Felix (twenties)

> Felix, an Asian-American man, speaks to Masha, a lost, lonely, lovely girl.

FELIX: That. That is the silky smooth hand of pan-Asian ancestry. Wisdom passed down from the gentle philosophies of Confucius and Lao-Tzu and . . . all those other guys. 'Cause I'm limber like a kung fu master, patient like a tai chi warrior and that guy who spent six years under the bodhi tree. You'll see the rewards of that patience, baby. I'll be ninja master all night long, I'll sneak about and cast so much mystery over your body that you can't stand waiting for what's behind my kabuki mask. And then I'll turn Bruce Lee crazy, mack daddy of the twirling rod and staff, and you'll feel the power of my jump and chop and kick, the fear and magic that pours sweaty force from me to you. 'Cause I'm samurai fierce, and if you want man, then I got four thousand years of warrior running through my blood, and it doesn't stop 'til it's reached that full-on, transcendental trance of enlightenment, like the angel heaven of a meditative master of man. I'm a mad Mongol machine, a cool kind of calm peninsular harbor just jutting its jaunty way in the sweet salty sea. So why don't you get on my body right about now . . . and I'll show you all the ancient secrets that lurk in the exotic flava of me.

The Mayor's Limo
Mark Nassar

Dramatic

Matty (early fifties)

> Matty is a police detective, closing in on early retirement. Here he is talking to a homeless guy brought in for peeing on the mayor's limousine about what his life is like on a daily basis.

MATTY: Yeah, it'll be real nice. I did all right by the department, but it'll be nice to have a change . . . after thirty years . . . Shit . . . shit . . . and more shit. There's plenty of it out there . . . thirty years . . . it's hard to believe . . . how many situations . . . how many collars. And I knew after the first arrest it was gonna be bullshit. *(Laughs, pause.)* I'm workin' the midnight to eight. Somewhere up around 138th Street . . . Brown Place . . . Brook Avenue. The real shit. It was a little before four in the morning and I wanted to get my meal before all the scumbags came outta the bars. So, I go to this place called the Doral. Good place to go when ya had no place to go. I get a booth in the back. I'm so tired I doze off. This guy starts shakin' me, saying: "There's a guy out there shootin' people." And the fuckin' guy says it so calm, like it's an everyday fuckin' occurrence. I'm like . . . Holy Shit. I wanted to crawl under the table. I wanted to call the fuckin' cops. But, I knew I had to go out there. Right in the middle of the intersection there's like fifty Puerto Ricans in black raincoats. I'm shittin' my pants, but I start toward them. I got my gun out. There's some Irish lady up in the window yelling: "Don't go over there, they got guns." They hear her and then they see me and then they start running into this bar carrying the people who got shot. They're running . . . I might as well run, too. But, not too fast. They all get into the bar. And I'm like, "Hang on a second, I'm not goin' in there." You're not supposed to go in with out backup. That rule never made more sense. There's a call box about a half a block. I'm so fucked up, I still got my gun out as I'm running toward the box. As I reach the corner and I'm starting to cross . . . there's a guy . . . I didn't see him . . . he's running from the other side of the street. He says: "Don't shoot I give up. Don't shoot me. I'm the guy who shot the people around the corner." Holy Shit. I say: "Take the gun out and empty it." Stupid move. You don't just let a guy take his gun out. He could of blown me away and nobody would've known boo. I tell him to stand against the wall. I go to the call box, . . . "I'm on post thirty-three, there's been a shooting." They say, "Hold on?" They hang up. What the fuck? Now, there's Puerto Ricans gathering all around me. It's starting to look like Custard's Last Stand. All of a sudden the Calvary comes over the hill. It's like fifty radio cars . . . sirens blasting. It was a scene. Sergeant pulls up to me . . . says: "What happened?" "I got this guy who shot the people." "Where is he?" "Against the wall." "Where?" "Right there against the wall." Sergeant says: "Well put the cuffs on him, put the fuckin' cuffs on him." I forgot to put the cuffs on. That's how nervous . . . So I cuffed 'em and we put 'em in the car. Sergeant says: "Relax, you did a good job. Now, what happened?" So, I say, ya know: "I really didn't catch this guy. The guy gave himself up. I didn't know . . . . ." Sergeant says: "Fuck 'em. Anybody asks you, you tell 'em you chased the mother-fucker three blocks." "I can't." He says: "Shut up. I'll take care of it when we get back to the station." That was it. I got a medal for some-thing . . . I didn't know what I was doing. The guy could've run by me and I would've run by him and it would've been nothing. They made a big deal. They gave me three days off. I got a big commen-dation. It was all bullshit. That was my first arrest. *(Pause.)* The sad part about it was, I went home and told my wife what a hero I was.

The Mayor's Limo
Mark Nassar

Comic

Benny (Banzai) Lambo (twenties to thirties)

>Benny is a homeless guy brought in by the cops for peeing on the mayor's limousine.

BANZAI: I got a little worked up before. I apologize for that. I ain't used to bein' locked up. I never played football in high school. I didn't win All-County either. I was just bustin' chops. But, I would still bet the Jets. That was no lie. All right. All right. *(Pause.)* Well, first of all, I didn't know it was the Mayor's limo. I mean there's these skels havin' a protest. And they're gettin' into it — chanting, the whole works. I don't even know what the fuck's goin' on. I'm just cruisin' down the street when I see all of this . . . lookin' for a place to take a piss. This guy Sammy I know . . . he's the ringleader. He tells me what's goin' on . . . The church don't want the men's shelter goin' in across the street and the bums are protesting . . . blah, blah, blah. I say to Sammy: "What the fuck do you expect? If the churchgoers gotta walk by all these bums on their way to church, they won't have no change left to throw in the basket when it comes around." I'm makin' a joke. *(Laughs.)* Sammy gets all bent outta shape . . . tells me I'm a hypocrite, calls me an asshole. I say: "Look at you, you little wimp, I'll show you how to have a protest." I was lookin' for a place to take a piss anyway. So I slip through the barriers and take a leak on this limo. I didn't know the Mayor was there. Sammy starts goin' crazy. He gets all the other skels screamin' and yellin': "We want shelter. We want shelter." It was a scene. I turn around in the middle of my leak and there's the whole gang comin' outta the church . . . the Mayor, the priests, some nuns. That's when Officer of the Year tackles me . . . thinks he's Joe Mannix, Private Eye. I thought I'd get a fine, not all this bullshit.

The Nina Variations
Steven Dietz

Dramatic

Treplev (twenties)

> This play is a fascinating series of riffs on Chekhov's *The Seagull*, involving only Konstantin Treplev and Nina. Here, Treplev is addressing the audience.

Treplev alone.

TREPLEV: There are buckets of love here. Dorn the doctor — of whom we would expect exactness — blames all this love on the lake; some quiet spell which has overtaken us. *(Treplev pauses, then looks at the audience, smiling.)* I often go to the theater. And when I do, I often spend the early part of the play saying to myself: "What in the world is *going on?!*" *(Treplev lifts a book — Chekhov's* The Seagull *— and shows it to the audience, buoyantly.)* To avoid such confusion tonight, I will now tell you *everything you need to know:* A group of people have gathered at a house near a lake. They are full of life and unlucky in love. *(He opens the book and refers to it.)* Polina Andreyevna — she loves Dorn, the doctor. But, sadly, she is married to Shamrayev, the retired army man. Medvedenko, the teacher, loves Masha. But, Masha loves *me.* (Which — despite everything else, black moods and clothing and all the rest — is, in its way, a sweet kindness.) For my part: I love Nina. But, Nina loves Trigorin. (And, worse, *Mother also loves Trigorin* — which is something we'll say no more about.) And as for Trigorin . . . he loves them all. And loves none of them well. I hate him for that. And for his success as a writer. And for his shallow charm, cunning smile and melancholic pose. And for making Nina bear his child out of wedlock. And, worse than hating him . . . I envy him all of it. *(He closes the book, abruptly. Looks at the audience.)* There you are. There's nothing more.

No Niggers, No Jews, No Dogs

John Henry Redwood

Dramatic

Yaveni (sixties)

> Yaveni, a Jewish man and friend of the Cheeks family, a black family in a small town in North Carolina, here talks about going through Kristallnacht in Germany.

YAVENI: *(Angered.) Kristallnacht!* "Night of broken glass." *(Pause.)* November 9, 1938, Nazis wearing swastika armbands began breaking the windows out of synagogues and temples, burning Torahs and killing Jews. Over ninety Jews were murdered that one night. All of this was happening while I . . . the *goy,* was having a dinner party at his home. At the party I was treated to the usual jokes. *(Mimicking.)* "You know how to get rid of all the niggers and kikes at the same time? Round up all the niggers and tie a dollar bill around their necks and put them on a boat back to Africa. Then the Jews will follow and stay there until get every one of those dollar bills." I was the only one not laughing. I could still see that colored man squirming and groaning on the ground. *(Pause.)* And I could still hear my voice scream "nigger." Mildred wanted to know what was the matter. *(Reflective.)* I got up and climbed the stairs to our bedroom. I reached way in the back of my closet and pulled out the large envelope containing the yarmulke Uncle Moishe had sent me. I put it on my head and went downstairs and sat at the table. While every eye in the house was on me, I cradled a piece of bread in my hand, and from the deep recesses of my being, I prayed a prayer I hadn't prayed in decades, the *Motzi,* the blessing for bread. *(Recites in Hebrew.) Baruch ata Adonai Elohainu melech ha'olam hamotzi lechem min ha'aretz.* Then I began to eat. After they recovered from being stunned, the guests began to excuse themselves, leaving shocked and confused. Mildred's brother came over to me and said, "If I had my shotgun, I'd blow your damned head off, you lying Jew son of a bitch." Mildred slowly went upstairs and came down with two suitcases. She stopped in front of me and quietly said, "I'm glad that Jew baby you put in me died." Then she walked out. That was the last time I saw the woman I loved . . . the woman I became a *goy* for *(Yaveni breaks down. Silence.)*

Omnium Gatherum
Theresa Rebeck and
Alexandra Gersten-Vassilaros

Dramatic

Khalid (forties to sixties)

> Khalid, a well-known Middle Eastern scholar, is a guest at a strange
> dinner party, which may be taking place in Hell (then again maybe
> not). Here he is addressing a late-arriving mystery guest, an Al Qaeda
> terrorist named Muhammed who, of course, believes that the only
> solution to the intractable Middle East problem is the use of vio-
> lence.

KHALID: *(To Mohammed.)* Who are you speaking to? Do you think you
are speaking to me? To these people, you have already said you have
nothing but contempt for them, you want to destroy them. So I ask
you, are you speaking to me? You are alienating the group you are
fighting for. This is what I want to ask you. If you get to the place
that you want, the land of milk and honey, how will you be able to
forget how you got there? Can you kill and slaughter your way into
heaven? And if you get in, then, that way, do you really belong there?
I ask you something. I ask you to answer me, as a fellow Arab. I ask
you to explain. Because I tell you, we can find peace through nego-
tiation, with the other peoples of the world, our neighbors, or we
can find peace by killing off all our enemies. Both will bring peace.
(Beat.) But which is peace?

Omnium Gatherum

Theresa Rebeck and
Alexandra Gersten-Vassilaros

Dramatic

Khalid (forties to sixties)

> Khalid, a respected Middle Eastern scholar, is at a dinner party which
> may be taking place in a kind of Hell. He has been provoked to anger
> by the late arrival of a guest who's an Al Qaeda terrorist, and he
> addresses this terrorist, the host, and the other guests.

KHALID: Nothing is fine! Is this the end? Is this all we have made of ourselves? Look at the world! We have created a world in which only
the most amoral behavior, whatever makes a dollar, whatever sells,
whatever tastes good, whatever feels good, that is what is promoted!
And that, that is the logic of the pornographer! It is the logic of the
child pornographer, who abandons all human feeling, who corrupts
the world for his own emptiness! Who destroys the children — No!
Look at what you do to the children! What you teach them! The in-
nocence you destroy! You know it is true! And why, why is it when
anyone speaks about the power of love it's suddenly an esoteric conversation!? No! No! You who talk so well must learn to listen! We
haven't got a lot of time to evolve here! This will be a compassion-
ate universe or it will cease becoming altogether! Let America strive
to become the, the size of a true hero, like our friend the firefighter!
Let her assistance be brave and supernatural!
(Hitting table.) The action of love, my silly friend, the action of
love. Forgive me, you're not silly. Not entirely. You're just hungry too,
aren't you? Aren't we all? Oh, I'm so depressed. I wish I had no brain,
just a heart the size of a giant fruit, then I would feed us all. I would.
I would feed us all.

The Pavilion
Craig Wright

Dramatic

Peter (thirties)

> Peter, attending his high school reunion, runs into old flame Kari, still the love of his life, to whom he is talking here.

PETER: Listen. You get this much time in your one life, right? Like you said, with your body, only this much. And you get this many people. Only this many. And out of the time and the people you're given you make what you make, and that's your life, right? But what if there's such a thing as destiny, do you ever think about that? But what if there is in the sense that, what if there was a person who could unlock the key to your life precisely because of what you did to them or what they did to you, or because you were stupid like me and you just missed it the first time around? Destiny like that, nothing cosmic. What if . . . what if it's like life, where when you're young you think it's gonna be about a lot of things and you prepare yourself for it, thinking, "Life is gonna be so wild, there's gonna be so much coming at me from every direction, how will I ever keep up?" That's what I always thought, and let me tell you, I sat down all ready to get my hair blown back by this explosion of millions of experiences that never ever came. And so the question becomes, what if you open your eyes after that and there's suddenly just one person, and it turns out that in some sense your entire life is really all about what you're gonna do about this one person and then what if you made a mistake? Are you telling me there's only one chance? The whole world exists so that everyone gets just one chance? One chance is enough of a reason to make a whole world? You're telling me there's no mercy, there's no forgiveness, there's no air in the system to breathe and no room to move and we're just trapped in the net of what we've done forever? Look, I was young and I was scared and I made a mistake. A big mistake. And I know it hasn't cost me what it cost you to live without that baby, but it's cost me a lot. It has. And when I look at you now, Kari, and I see those little wrinkles around your eyes . . . ? And I realize I've missed so much of you already . . . ? The thought that I won't see the rest, that I won't get to know you any better and hold your hand and see your smile . . . and then one day you'll be gone forever? That breaks my heart. I can't live any further into my life without *you*. Please. Come back to The Cities with me tonight. Get a divorce. Marry me. Or live with me. Or let's have another baby and just be friends, I don't care, let's . . . just . . . come on. We'll start over. Look, whatever we've done, both our lives are a mess, right? A mess! And I've got a car and a full tank of gas. *(After a beat.)* Are you coming?

The Pavilion
Craig Wright

Dramatic

Peter (thirties)

> Peter, while attending his high school reunion, runs into his first love, Kari. He also runs into his old buddy Smoke, with whom he is commiserating here.

PETER: It's like when I said no to Kari back then, when I left town? It's like I got on the wrong train, you know? And I've been on this train now for twenty years, and Jesus, I don't want to go where this train is going. I really don't. I want to go . . . I want to go where I maybe could have gone with her, you know? . . . if I had been more . . . I don't know, strong or something. When I saw Kari for the first time, Smoke, I'll never forget it; it was like the first or second week of high school and I walked into the audiovisual lab and there she was. And I swear — I couldn't have put this into words back then, but it's all I think about lately — it was really like I recognized her or something. And I don't mean it like we'd met before or anything. We'd never met. It was just . . . it was as if in her face . . . in her beauty . . . I was finally seeing the beauty of everything, you know? . . . the unreachable beauty of the whole world that I'd always felt inside and tried to hold onto but never could, it was all in her. The whole universe had articulated itself in her. To me. That's just how I saw it. And I just knew that if I could be with her . . . by her side, you know? . . . then I could be alive and be a part of things. I'd at least have a chance. Now I know it sounds crazy, Smoke, I know, given everything that's happened, and there's a lot of water gone under the bridge, and a lot of time has passed, and there's been a lot of stupid shit and I've done most of it, but when I see her now, I still feel the same way. I look at her and I still see it, I see her face and I think, "Oh, there you are . . . the world. Where have you been?" I love her, you know? I screwed up back then, there's no getting around it, but I love her. I think she's great. I love her.

The Potato Creek Chair of Death

Robert Kerr

Dramatic

Michael (seventeen)

> Michael is a teenage fugitive from Ohio seeking a legendary "chair
> of death." In this monologue, he confesses to Valerie, an elderly
> woman with whom he has forged a connection, why he is on the
> run from the law.

MICHAEL: Finding you wasn't part of the plan. No. I don't mean that. You
must have been a part of the plan I didn't know about. The plan for
my life. What I'm meant to do. I feel like I'm reading the signs all
wrong. It wasn't me that killed my parents, right? It was the universe.
I was just a tool. They were meant to die. I just did what the signs
said I should do. I mean, when I got up at two in the morning and
I was really thirsty so I went downstairs and I was looking for the
orange juice pitcher, it was a sign when I opened the cupboard where
Mom kept the rat poison. I wasn't thinking about it. I just opened
it by mistake. Except it wasn't a mistake because the universe does
things like that — gets in your brain and makes you do things. I
didn't know right away what I should do with the poison. But I knew
it was either them or me. I had to make sure I did the right thing,
so I made the orange juice and poured it into two cups that looked
exactly the same and put the poison in one of them. I closed my eyes
and switched them around a bunch of times and spun myself around
so I was really dizzy. I kept my eyes closed and took one of the cups
and drank it. I felt kind of sick, but I didn't know if I drank the one
with the poison so I poured the other cup back into the pitcher and
went to bed. I couldn't fall asleep right away, but I didn't feel as sick
after a while. Then I thought maybe I should tell my parents about

the poison. But it was like too much trouble to get them up at three in the morning. I turned off the alarm because if I woke up on my own time I was meant to save their lives. I fell asleep and I dreamed about the Chair of Death which I heard about in second grade. I woke up and I wasn't . . . So they were . . . I got the car. I started driving. I knew I had to find the Chair of Death because I had that dream about it. And now I feel like I'm Charles Manson or something, because I guess compared to other parents mine weren't all that bad. They never hit me. They never grabbed for my crotch. They never did anything. I never did anything. We all just sat around doing nothing. It was like we were all already dead, so what difference does it make if I really did kill them, right?

Q.E.D.
Peter Parnell

Seriocomic

Feynman (fifties)

> Physicist Richard Feynman (played by Alan Alda in the original New
> York production) is here talking to a student named Miriam, telling
> her about how he won the Nobel prize.

FEYNMAN: Miriam, I'm sorry. I didn't mean to be rough on you. See, Nature has been dancing with me all my life. She's tantalized me, and
sometimes I feel like I've gotten so close to her . . . close enough to
lift her veil . . . but now I feel like I'm finished . . . I'm done for . . .
I haven't felt like this since . . . There was one other time. It was after
the War. I was offered a job teaching at Cornell, and as I began to
teach the course something wasn't right. Suddenly, when I tried to,
I just couldn't get to work! It was driving me crazy! From the war,
and my first wife's death . . . And everything else . . . I had worked
so hard on the bomb . . . I had simply . . . burned myself out . . .
Well, finally I thought to myself, This is impossible to live up to —
therefore, don't live up to it! You used to enjoy physics, I said to myself. Why not enjoy it again? Why not PLAY with it?! AMUSE
YOURSELF! HAVE FUN! Yeah . . . So within a week of feeling this
way, I was in the school dining hall, when all of a sudden . . . Some
guy was fooling around. He throws a plate in the air. One of those
plates with the university seal on one rim. As the plate goes up, I see
it wobble, and I notice the red medallion going around, and it's pretty
obvious that the plate's wobble is faster than its spin. I figure out the
motion. See, when the angle is very slight, the wobble is twice as fast
as the spin — two to one. It turns out to be a pretty complicated
equation! I tell Hans Bethe, and he says, "That's interesting, Feynman, but what's the IMPORTANCE of it?" And I say, "It HAS no
importance! It's just for FUN!" But see, here's the thing, I went on

working out various equations of wobbles. Then I thought about how electron orbits start to move in relativity, and about the path of least time in Q.E.D., and before I knew it, I was playing — working, really — in the same old way I used to . . . It was like uncorking a bottle. And a lot of what I got the Nobel Prize for, years later, came out of piddling around with that wobbling plate! *(He laughs.)*

Safe
Tony Glazer and Anthony Ruivivar

Comic

Evan (twenties)

> Evan is one of a group of people locked in a bank vault during a robbery. Here, he tells the other lock-ins why he has a deathly fear of puppets.

EVAN: On my fifth birthday, my folks threw a big party. They were having problems, and I guess they felt they could make it up to me with clowns, ponies, and ice cream cake. The main event was *Freddy and Pickles*, a ventriloquist act. Pickles was his dummy and he dressed him like a . . . a Hasidic Jew. You know with the black hat and coat. He even had the curly hair twirling down the side of his little hat. I was mesmerized. To me, Pickles was as real as any other kid, and he made me laugh. So I took him. I waited 'til they finished the act, and while Freddy was getting some cake, I popped open his box and hid the little Jewish puppet in my room. I had him for weeks. I brought him food and water, but he never touched it. I thought it was part of his religion. We had a great time. Then one day I decided we'd go play in the yard. It was Sunday, so I thought it would be okay, it being God's day and all. I loved to create little make-believe scenarios, like Lost in the Jungle, Space Planet Seven, or sometimes I'd just take off his pants and dance him around. My mom called me in for lunch from the house. She didn't know about Pickles, so my plan was to leave him in the tall grass and when I was done with lunch go back outside, get him, and sneak him back to my room. I was halfway through my jelly sandwich when I heard the lawn mower. I froze. If I made a move and ran for him, the gig would be up, and if I stayed and finished my sandwich, Pickles would die. It took me like three days to find all of him. A wood chip here. A wood chip there. A little curl of hair. I killed my best friend. Then, on my sixth birthday, my parents took me to a puppet show. I took one look at that little stage, saw the shadow of a puppet just behind the little curtain, and freaked out. I couldn't stop shaking. I was terrified one of those little fuckers were going to exact their revenge for Pickles by strangling me with the wires they hang from. To this day, I can't . . . you know, go to theme parks or wax museums. I know now they're not real, but I believe in karma, and the fear of one of them going haywire and killing me still comes up. It's ridiculous, I know, but I'm convinced I will die at the hands of some type of puppet!

Sally's Gone, She Left Her Name
Russell Davis

Dramatic

Christopher (teens)

> Christopher is talking to his father about a disturbing dream he recently had.

CHRISTOPHER: Yeah, you told us what's real, Dad. It's our family. Nothing else at all has to be real. Anything else is just a phase, that's all, Dad. I promise you. Only a phase. *(Light focuses on Christopher.)* Cause I have them, Dad, myself. Lots of phases. And Sally, you see her. She's worse than the moon. How she sits out there on our lawn. In the middle of the night. When I get up to go to the bathroom. The first time I thought she was a sheet. I thought, that's weird. Who could have left that white sheet out there on our lawn? And then I thought, is that a dead body? It's a body, I bet, under that sheet. Who could have left that sheet over a dead body on our lawn? Until I realized, no. No, wait, that's Sally. That's my sister out there. In her white nightgown. I wonder should I go out and talk to her? But I decided to get back to bed. Get some sleep. But just as I was lying down I noticed I had an arrow in my chest. Somebody outside must have shot an arrow. Which came through my window and landed right where I was in bed. So I got up to go to the bathroom again to take this arrow out. Except I heard Dad downstairs in the kitchen. Talking to some people outside, telling them not to come in. But when I went downstairs, I could see nobody he was talking to. Then Dad asked what was wrong, and I told him about the arrow which somebody shot in my chest. But he couldn't see it, any arrow which came through my window. So I went to my room to get the arrow, but by then I saw my whole bed had arrows, sticking up on it, all over. I decided I better close this window. Except the wall was gone. The whole wall to our house. And I was standing on the edge of my room holding just the window. And while I held the window, I saw that white sheet again. Caught up there in a tree. Flapping in the wind. And then I saw at my feet there was a ditch, which had water. Which then got deeper and wider. Like a moat. And I saw the sheet in the tree across the water get further and further away from me, accelerating, until it became like a star in the night. And I was standing there, looking at this star, when I heard somebody call out behind me. They called, "Good-bye." But when I looked back, I saw our house was gone. The whole house. I couldn't tell anymore it was ever there. *(Pause.)* Mom? *(Pause.)* Mom? Is that you? Did you call, Mom, good-bye? Was that you?

Shoot
David Cirone

Dramatic

Mr. Malcolm (thirty-two)

> Mr. Malcolm, a high school teacher, explains to his colleague his regret at sleeping with a student.

MR. MALCOLM: You think I go looking for this? You know how it is, to be my age, there at that school . . . It's constant. Constantly, day after day . . . ! I mean, these aren't "girls" anymore, you know? These are women. Young women, wearing God knows what! They didn't dress like this, or talk like this back when I was . . . we're talking ten, twelve years ago? I'm thirty-two years old, and they're like fucking sharks on me! All day I got breasts in my face! All day! The hands, the fingers touching me . . . ! They still wanna give me these warm hugs, you know, "friendly" hugs, but . . . what am I gonna do? Not care? Shut them out? Cut myself off? How can I do that? I spend so much time with these kids! It's like I'm their father, or their big brother . . . And yeah — yeah, I like being the cool teacher, yeah I smoke across the street with the kids sometimes, and you know, there's this — there's this bond. I mean, I care for them. I know them. I know them better than their parents do, if they even have parents! You know what I mean — you get this trust, and you want that trust and you want that connection and you want it to be real — no bullshit, none of that fake shit you always got from your parents and your teachers when you were a kid . . . And so . . . and so, yeah — the line gets blurry sometimes. And I think — with her — it got . . . erased. It just somehow got erased . . . *(Pause.)* I really care about her. Like, I'm glad that I can see her, see her as a person. I know she needs that. Her parents — have you met her parents? At open house they talk about her like she's not even there. Like she's this thing. And so it starts out that I'm just happy I can give her that appreciation, and then our connection was so natural, it just grew . . .

Speaking in Tongues
Andrew Bovell

Dramatic

Leon (thirties to forties)

> Leon is speaking to his wife, Sonya, about a disturbing encounter
> he had while out jogging.

LEON: About four or five days ago, I think it was about Wednesday, I was
running down this hedge. And I'd built up this tremendous speed.
I could feel the force of my body. I hadn't run like that since I was
a boy. You know, just completely let go. I could feel the blood pump-
ing through my body and my muscles tightening and the veins in
my neck bursting . . . it was exhilarating. But just as I reached the
end of the hedge a man came around the corner and SMACK —
(He claps his hands together.) I ran straight into him. Yeah it was funny
but it was shocking too, like being in a car accident. And anyway I
let forth with this most amazing torrent of abuse . . . "You fucking
idiot. Why don't you fucking look where you're going. You fucking
arsehole." And I don't know where this is coming from, but I keep
it up for . . . it feels like ages, but I guess it was only seconds. But
I'm screaming at this guy. And it's not because I'm angry at him because really —

   Yes, it was my fault. But, I think, I'm screaming at this guy, not
because I'm angry at him, but because I think I've lost you. I think
some stupid indiscretion with a stranger has cost me the most im-
portant thing in my life. And he's there, right in my face, so I'm
screaming at him . . . when I notice that's he cowering. He's got his
hands up over his face and he's cowering, like a dog being beaten.
This grown man is cowering because of me. He thinks I'm going to
hit him. So I stop and I take stock and I say, "I'm sorry. I'm sorry.
Here, let me help you." And I pull him up and I see that I've smashed
the guy's nose in. With my head. With my hard stupid fat head, I've

broken this man's nose. There's blood all over his face. "I'm sorry. Are you all right? Let me help you." But he pushes me away and he says, "No, I'm fine. I'm fine. Please." And he walks off down the hedge. But I can see he's not fine and I just feel terrible, so I follow him. He turns the corner. And I hear him, I don't see him, I hear him stop and he starts to weep. The man has completely broken down and he's weeping. I mean, what makes a man weep like that?

String Fever
Jacquelyn Reingold

Seriocomic

Gisli (forty-four)

> Gisli, an Icelandic comedian and actor, is in a rehab center in
> America, where he runs into Matthew, the ex-husband of his friend
> Lily. Here, he tells Matthew, who has real problems himself, about
> how he wound up in rehab.

GISLI: It's very simple Matt, I slipped I fell I fucked up, and Inge left, so
now I get up I go after her and if along the way I fall I get up again
until each time it is easier to get up and soon I hope falling is no
longer necessary I can just skip the falling and keep the getting up
that's all. Without Inge the world is for shit. And I am famous in
my country I am like David Letterman famous, I can have girls a
lot of girls and let me tell you Icelandic girls are most beautiful forget California, in Iceland we walk around with a hard-on we are sick
from the gorgeous girls, all day it's very inconvenient, but the point
is they are nothing next to my Inge. Who is OK past forty years old,
who does not have this perfect body anymore. But she is my other
me. But I am stupid human being so I fuck up all the time every
day my dick wants me to follow it around into beautiful young girls
and sometimes I go, like dick dick dick I follow you, dick dick, I
agree my wife is getting old, dick dick, I do anything you want, but
I know better I am forty-four years old and I know better!!! I know
if I pick up a drink I am drunk. I know if I lose my wife less than
half of me is left. These stupid therapists say I am codependent, she
is codependent fuck you nothing wrong with dependent. It means
I am lucky I found her. I thank God for that. It also means I am
human and I push her away. So now I must try to get her back. So
first I stop drinking and then I throw myself at her feet and beg she
can forgive and if she says no I beg again, I keep at it til she either

tells me to never come to her again or she takes me back stupid idiot
I am. And I try my best to remember and not forget that she is everything to me. Every day. You don't see anything Matt. You're not even
looking. What are you doing here? Sucking up more group therapy?
How old are you? Fifteen? Twenty? Past forty aren't you? Tick tock
Matt, the clock waits for no one. It's half over if you're lucky. Stop
tugging at your own dick and thinking you're doing something. Who
cares what your feelings are? Feeling shmeeling? You can spend the
next ten years getting in touch with your feelings and then you'll be
past fifty, and you'll still be an idiot. Get over it. Grow up, Matt.

String Fever
Jacquelyn Reingold

Dramatic

Matthew (about forty)

> Matthew, a guy with big problems, tries to tell Lily, his ex-wife, what it's been like without her.

MATTHEW: I go to the drugstore for my medication, and the pharmacist is chatting and chatting with someone, so I raise my voice, he yells at me, I storm out and accidentally on purpose slam the door and it cracks the glass, I call to apologize, but next day the police come and give me a summons. At the hearing the DA recommends they put me away forever because, he says, it's my third strike, he says, I'm a two-time felon, and my lawyer who I found in the Yellow Pages, looks at me with this why-didn't-you-tell-me-what-else-haven't-you-told-me kind of look and there is so much I wouldn't know where to begin. Should I tell him how there hasn't even been a me for two years? But I'm in court for slamming a door so I say nothing, besides, in a way he's right. I have struck out. I know I asked you to leave, I did, but Lily Lil where I was heading I didn't want to bring you. And the judge looks at his papers and says, "Are you Matthew Houseman born in 1955?" And I say no, I was born in '59. They realize it's another Matthew Houseman. And the lawyer sighs. The judge smiles. It's a mistake. All I have to do is pay a fine. Which makes no sense whatsoever without you.

Take Me Out
Richard Greenberg

Seriocomic

Mason (thirties to forties)

> Mason is a middle-aged gay man, a financial manager, who has been given the job of managing the money of a baseball superstar who has recently revealed to the press and to his teammates that he is gay. Mason, who knew nothing about baseball, figured he should learn something about it by going to some games — and he's become completely hooked.

MASON: So I've done what was suggested. I continued to watch, and I have come (with no little excitement) to understand that baseball is a perfect metaphor for hope in a democratic society.

It has to do with the rules of play.

It has to do with the mode of enforcement of these rules.

It has to do with certain nuances and grace notes of the game.

First, it's the remarkable symmetry of everything.

All those threes and multiples of three, calling attention to — virtually making a *fetish* of — the game's noble equality.

Equality, that is, of opportunity.

Everyone is given exactly the same chance.

And the opportunity to exercise that chance at his own pace.

There's none of that scurry, none of that relentlessness, that marks other games — basketball, football, hockey.

I've never watched basketball, football, or hockey, but I'm sure I wouldn't like them. Or maybe I would, but it wouldn't be the same.

What I mean is, in baseball there's no clock.

What could be more generous than to give everyone all these opportunities and the time to seize them in as well? And with each turn at the plate, there's the possibility of turning the situation to your favor. Down to the very last try.

And then, to ensure that everything remains fair, justices are ranged around the park to witness and assess the play.

And if the justice errs, an appeal can be made.

It's invariably turned down, but that's part of what makes the metaphor so right.

Because even in the most well-meant of systems, error is inevitable. Even within the fairest of paradigms, unfairness will creep in.

And baseball is better than democracy — or at least than democracy as it's practiced in this country — because, unlike democracy, baseball acknowledges loss.

While conservatives tell you, "Leave things alone and no one will lose," and liberals tell you, "Interfere a lot and no one will lose," baseball says, "Someone will lose." Not only *says* it — insists upon it!

So that baseball achieves the tragic vision democracy evades. Evades *and* embodies.

Democracy is lovely, but baseball's more mature.

(Pause.)

Another thing I like is the home-run trot.

Not the mad dash around the bases when it's an inside-the-ballpark home run — I'm not sure I've ever *seen* an inside-the-ballpark home run — I'm talking about that graceful little canter when the ball has been crushed, and it's missing, and the outcome's not in doubt.

What I like about it is it's so unnecessary.

The ball's gone, no one's going to bring it back. And can anyone doubt that a man capable of launching a ball four hundred feet is somehow going to *fail* to touch a base when he's running uninterfered with?

For all intents and purposes, the game at that moment, is not being played.

If duration of game is an issue — and I'm given to believe that duration of game *is* an issue — the sensible thing would be to say, yes, that's gone, add a point to the score, and send the next batter to the plate.

But that's not what happens.

Instead, play is suspended for a celebration.

A man rounds four bases, and if he's with the home team, the crowd has a catharsis.

And from the way he runs, you learn something about the man. And from the way they cheer, you learn something about the crowd.

And I like this because I don't believe in God.

Or — well — don't *know* about God. Or about any of that . . . metaphysical murk.

Yet I like to believe that something about being human is . . . good.

And I think what's best about us is manifested in our desire to show respect for one another. For what we can be.

And that's what we do in our ceremonies, isn't it?

Honor ourselves as we pass through time?

And it seems to me that to conduct this ceremony not before a game or after a game but in the very *heart* of a game is . . . quite . . . well, does any other game do that?

That's baseball.

Take Me Out
Richard Greenberg

Seriocomic

Mason (late thirties to forties)

> Mason is a middle-aged, gay, financial advisor who has recently been given the job of managing Darren Lemming's money. Darren, a baseball superstar, has recently "outed" himself to his teammates and to the press. The resulting controversy has made him seriously consider quitting baseball. Mason, who has become intoxicated by baseball (and, let's be frank, just a little bit with Darren) tries to explain to the recalcitrant superstar why he can't quit.

MASON: I have been watching baseball nonstop since the day I was told you were coming to me. And at first it was a chore. I understood nothing. I couldn't tell one player from another. And then I *could.* And it wasn't a chore any longer, it was . . . this . . . astonishment! This . . . *abundance.* So much to learn, so much to memorize . . .When you're not playing now, I watch whoever is; when there's no one playing, I watch tapes from twenty years ago; when I'm out of tapes, I read books. I've been *crying* for two months. That's a ridiculous, that's a disgusting, thing to say. I hate people who tell you how they're *crying.* "Oh, I'm so deep — it's so meaningful — I *cried.*" Bullshit. I'm telling you *because* it's ludicrous — I *know* it's ludicrous. But Darren, I *never* cry about *any*thing. I only ever have about *two* feelings a year; and all of a sudden . . . *(He spreads his arms, speechless.)* I'm having *memories.* Playing catch with Dad. Going to games over summer vacation. They're not even *my memories,* but I'm *having* them. I don't get it. I don't get any of it. I don't know why I feel exalted when we win. I don't know why I feel diminished when we lose. I don't know why I'm saying "we" . . . ! Life is so . . . tiny, so *daily.* This . . . you . . . take me out of it . . . I know . . . things are hard for you now . . . I know it's a difficult time . . . but don't tell me you're *flat.* Be in agony, but don't be indifferent. Look where we are! Smell the air!

Till We Meet Again
Colin and Mary Crowther

Comic

Teenager (a teenager)

> A teenaged boy (could be a girl, I guess) talks about the trials and tribulations of puberty.

TEENAGER: Oh no! It's happening again. I'm sweating. Do you know the first thing I'll do? When I know everything? I'll invent a cure for puberty. *(He breaks Down Right.)* No more flushes and blushes and gallons of sweat and stink and . . . things. I'll be able to say, "You are my body and you are under my control. You are my brain and you will think what I tell you, when I tell you, and *you will never embarrass me on public transport again!" (He begins to break to Down Center.)* And when someone says — oh, something clever and cutting — I'll be able to come back with just the right words. Kapow! And I'll be smooth and cool and . . . and not sweaty and sticky and covered in zits! Do you know my greatest fear? That one day someone will squeeze me — and I'm so oily and sweaty and sticky — I'll just go *pfit* and pop out of my shirt — my whole body will pop out of my clothes and up in the air and I'll be up there in full view of everyone — stark bullock naked — and they'll all laugh! Because they don't understand. No one understands . . . what it's like . . . to be me!

To Fool the Eye

Jeffrey Hatcher

An adaptation of Jean Anouilh's Leocadia

Comic

Prince Albert (twenties to thirties)

> The prince lives in a chateau presided over by an eccentric duchess, who hopes to make him forget about the death of his great love, Leocadia. Here he is talking to Amanda, a poor hatmaker, who has been brought to the chateau by the duchess to assist her in dispelling Albert's thoughts of suicide.

PRINCE: *(His voice stops her.)* Mademoiselle! I know I am of a class from which the grand comic tradition of farce recruits its stock characters, its frauds and fools. I was raised in a world of old ladies and retainers and never had much, if any, contact with what you might call . . . life. I was born to limitations, and if that warrants calling me a fool, fine! Go ahead! Call me a fool! But know this: A fool is just a name for someone you don't understand. Your type sit in cafés and complain about the oppression of the masses, but I'll wager it's never occurred to you that a prince can be oppressed! Do you know what it's like to grow up in a monument to the sixteenth century? Do you know what it's like to have twenty-two names accompanied by a series of titles that lost all significance before the invention of the belt buckle? Every time I went into Dinard the children mocked me behind my back, for the way I walked and bowed and tipped my hat. Find a village idiot and discover he can spell, they give him a scholarship and make him President of the Republic, but grow up an aristocrat and you have to be a genius just to stay on par!

Trip of a Lifetime
Bill Cashmore and Andy Powrie

Dramatic

Barry (thirties to forties)

> Barry is telling a woman named Sheila about the pain he felt when his wife left him.

BARRY: I know you can't understand how I've failed to sustain any sort of long-term relationship. But that's because you've found it so easy. You've been lucky. To find the love of your life in your teens, marry and live happily ever after. It just doesn't happen to most of us. I thought that Laura was my future. I was very happy with her, and I couldn't imagine a life without her. But when she left I wasn't given any choice. She'd made her mind up. *(Pause.)* I never told you exactly how it happened did I? It was Christmas Eve. Good timing, eh? We'd had Trevor and Christine over for drinks and it was a really nice evening. They went at about two o'clock on Christmas morning and Laura and I sat to have a final drink. She took a deep breath and said "You know there's something wrong don't you?" But I didn't. I thought everything was great. Then she said "I'm sorry but I'm leaving you, Barry." I asked her why and she said she couldn't see a future with me. It didn't matter what I said, she'd decided. *(Pause.)* Christmas Day was a bit of a muted affair. People were very supportive. Trevor and Christine. Trevor took a particular interest. We had a lot in common. He'd been seeing Laura for the best part of a year. I'm not sure if it was better or worse that she'd fallen in love with someone else. I suppose it was better. I think it would be worse if she'd just rather be on her own than with me. *(Pause.)* Anyway, I don't want to bore you anymore with it, but the point I'm making is that I did work at the relationship — I think I did. I tried. But if someone falls out of love with you — it's not your fault. It's no one's fault. It happens. And it happened to me.

The Why
Victor Kaufold

Dramatic

Robert (teens)

> Robert, a teenager, is speaking with a prison therapist after having perpetrated a school shooting.

ROBERT: Yeah. People in cars are . . . funny. It's like . . . they're exaggerations of what they're like in the real world. They're in this car, and it's like they're completely absorbed in their own little capsule. Nothing outside of the car matters unless it's going to affect their car. They just sit there completely focused on the red light waiting for it to turn green. I'm pretty sure the wish "Man, I hope this light turns green soon" is thought more often than "Man, I wish everyone on Earth could live together in peace." — Traffic light was invented by a black man. Did you know that? Well, some people, they're so wrapped up in their little car-related affairs, they don't notice anything. — Even things that are car-universe relevant, like, say, the light changing. Then, this of course sends the guy behind them, who seemed fine just one second ago, into a complete and total rage. And you can watch him go out of his mind and wave his arms around inside his little capsule. — And during this special period, a person could do any of a number of things to this upstanding citizen, and he would never be the wiser.

But I've forgotten the best part: The people who do notice me, but *pretend* not to. Those are by far the coolest. You know, I'll start doing something weird, and they'll notice, — but instantly, this reflex kicks in which tells them not to look. So they just try to sit there and get nervous because they realize that their capsule is in danger of collapsing. But then, the black man's invention turns green, and they're off, safe and never to be seen again. One out of every million people will notice me, but they're usually kids, and kids of course don't count.

OK. I took a gun into school, shot four kids, three of which died, and now I'm sitting here . . . It's weird but I can almost forget I did anything. Like look at it this way: Does the universe miss those three people I killed? Killing a person, I don't think is any different than killing an animal or chopping down a tree. Each one is going to upset certain people . . . but when you look at the big picture, is anything any different, did anything really change? No. How many people do you think have died on this Earth never doing one worthwhile thing their whole lives? The number must be in the fucking trillions . . . When I shot William Blackwell and Jamal Livingston and Jessica whatever-her-name-is and Alec . . . — I saw enough to know their lives were already wasted. They happened to be four wasted lives in easy shooting distance, that's all. Is that so hard to understand? I mean, OK: *William* was going to continue being an asshole and end up working like a slave to support a family that hates him, right? And Jamal . . . What? Honestly . . . A drug overdose? Stabbed to death by a jacket thief? Ms. Jessica . . . Well she was clearly going to end up being some mindless trophy wife for some exec guy who had about ten other trophies. And Alec . . . poor Alec wasn't gonna do anything. And neither was I. That's the one thing I learned at school. At least I don't have to worry about going back there . . . Same dirty hallways, same stupid faces. Same sounds. Regulations. Moving through the halls like cattle. Every day. There it was, right in your face. It sucked. I hated it. But now, well . . . Now I have new things to bother me. And this time they're all my fault. Alec didn't die. One of my bullets took off *his face* but he didn't die. Right now he's somewhere with hamburger meat for a face . . . *(Bell rings.)* Oh . . . Lunch time . . .

A Year in the Death of Eddie Jester

T. Gregory Argall

Seriocomic

Eddie (twenties to thirties)

> Eddie, a stand-up comic, has been mugged and is in a coma. While his body is comatose, though, Eddie roams the stage making wry observations "out of body."

EDDIE: . . . me. Here I am. Like the man said, I just won't go away. Not from a lack of trying, though. Who'd want to stay here? I mean look around. Take a real hard look at this place. At first glance it seems pretty nice, but I've had some time to check it all out. Not much else I can do and, hey, I figure I'm allowed, right? I mean this is the deep dark inside of my mind. If anyone's gonna snoop around, it should be me. You people can't. You're not even real. You're just part of my subconscious. Yeah. Think about it. Spooky, huh? So, anyway, like I was saying. This place looks fine on this side, but you should see backstage. Just a big empty room with a few boxes covered with duct tape and dust. A couple of mice huddled in the corner, crying, "Help me, help me!" There used to be a lot of light but it's pretty shadowy back there now. Luckily, I'm a happy-go-lucky kind of guy, so it doesn't bother me. No, really. It's a side effect of being a dyed-in-the-wool pessimist. I've given this a lot of thought. I know what I'm talking about. Take your average optimist, walking through life, "La-de-da, everything's going to work out fine and only good things will happen," and when good things do happen, he just takes it in stride, because he expected good things anyway, so it's nothing special. But when bad things happen, and they're bound to, eventually. Law of averages. When bad things happen, he's really bummed out. Seriously messed up, like the universe betrayed him or something. But with a pessimist, like, say . . . me, for instance, walking around seeing the downside of everything. If something goes wrong, well, yeah, I saw that coming, big deal. Get over it. But when things work out in your favor, something goes according to plan, when you win, damn, does that feel good. It's the greatest natural high, next to sex, of course, and pessimism plays a big part in that, too. A true pessimist will never quit. But an optimist. An optimist is three hundred times more likely to get depressed and kill himself. Sure, that's not a real statistic, it's just something I made up. But what the hell. My mind, my stats. *(Lights go up on hospital rooms; same old scene; bed, patient, fewer cards.)* Of course, none of this "pessimists are the real winners" crap changes the fact that I'm still lying there, waiting for God to flip a coin. Not even doing that rattle and hum stuff any more. Just lying there, not moving. They dust me every couple of nights. I'm not kidding. Some newbie intern drew the short straw and he has to go dust the comatose patients. They do it after visiting hours, of course, but still. Jesus. Out of all of this, that's the one thing that still really gives me the screaming heebie-jeebies, you know. Three o'clock. Time for sex.

You Could Die Laughing
Billy St. John

Comic

Antonio (twenties)

> Antonio, a streetwise stand-up comic, has been invited to a lodge by
> a mysterious billionaire and told he's to audition for a TV series. Here
> he's doing a "routine" for some of the other invitees, also comics.

ANTONIO: Yep. I've always had a smart mouth on me . . . *(Moving about
at will.)* . . . and whenever I get nervous, I tend to talk like a parrot
on uppers. Well, that day the smart-alec remarks came flying out of
me — and those goons started laughing. The more I talked, the more
they laughed. I figure it saved my skin — I mean, you're not gonna
beat up on somebody that makes you laugh, right? *(He goes into a
comic routine, "playing the room.")* "Hey, big fella, is that your head
or are you carrying a boulder on your shoulder? I'm Antonio, what's
your name? Jimmy Lee? Nice teeth, Jimmy Lee — all five of 'em! I
like your tattoos . . . By the way, *death* has an *a* in it! *Mom* is spelled
right, though. Homemade, huh? You really made those with a switch-
blade and a bottle of ink? And they say good penmanship is going
out of style. You did your own piercings, too, huh? How 'bout that?
It must be nice to know if you ever rip your pants, you have some
safety pins handy. Who are you? Buford? I wish I had hair like that,
Buford . . . but on my head instead 'a my back. If you ever run short
'a cash, you can shave it, weave it, and sell it as doormats." *(Drop-
ping the routine.)* You get the idea. By the time my mama wired the
bail money, my fellow felons and I were the best of friends . . . and
I had found my calling. Incidentally, that experience taught me a les-
son — that and my mama's flyswatter on my backside — and I never
took anything ever again. That includes Allen's missing key and the
cell phone batteries. If I'm lyin', I'm dyin'!

RIGHTS AND PERMISSIONS

ACTOR! © 2003 by Frederick Stroppel. Reprinted by permission of the author and Samuel French, Inc. Published in an acting edition by Samuel French, Inc., 45 W. 25th St., New York, NY 10010. Contact Samuel French, Inc. for performance rights.

APPOINTMENT WITH A HIGHWIRE LADY. © 2003 by Russell Davis. Reprinted by permission of Susan Gurman, Susan Gurman Agency, 865 West End Ave., New York, NY 10025-8403. Performance rights handled by Broadway Play Publishing, 56 E. 81 St., New York, NY 10028-8358. Published by Broadway Play Publishing in *Plays by Russell Davis*.

BEAUTY'S DAUGHTER. © 2003 by Dael Orlandersmith. Reprinted by permission of Random House, Inc. Published by Dramatists Play Service in *The Gimick & Other Plays*. Performance rights handled by Dramatists Play Service, 440 Park Ave. S, New York, NY 10016

BLACK THANG. © 2002 by Ato Essandoh. Reprinted by permission of the author. Published in *Plays and Playwrights 2003* by New York Theatre Experience Box 744, New York, NY 10274-0744. For performance rights, contact the author c/o New York Theatre Experience, via mail or via e-mail: info@botz.com

THE BOYS THEY LEFT BEHIND. © 2003 by Donald Steele. Reprinted by permission of the author. 2 Horatio St. #5C, New York, NY 10014. As of this printing, this play has not been published. Contact the author regarding performance rights or procurement of the complete text.

BROADWAY MACABRE. © 2003 by Don Nigro. Reprinted by permission of the author and Samuel French, Inc., 45 W. 25th St., New York, NY 10010. Published by Samuel French, Inc. in *DeFlores and Other Plays*. Contact Samuel French, Inc. for performance rights.

CAIRO. © 2001 by Arthur Melville Pearson. Reprinted by permission of Playscripts, Inc. Box 237060, New York, NY 10023. Contact publisher for performance rights or for a copy of the complete text: www.playscripts.com (Web site); info@playscripts.com (e-mail); 866-NEW-PLAY (phone)

CHAIN MAIL. © 2003 by Frederick Stroppel. Reprinted by permission of the author and Samuel French, Inc., 45 W. 25 St., New York, NY 10010. Published by Samuel French, Inc. in *Judgment Call and Other Plays*. Contact Samuel French, Inc. for performance rights.

CIRCUMFERENCE OF A SQUIRREL. © 2003 by John Walch. Reprinted by permission of Playscripts, Inc. For performance rights, or for a copy of the complete text, contact publisher: www.playscripts.com (Web site); info@playscripts.com (e-mail); 1-866-NEW-PLAY (phone).

CREATURES LURKING IN THE CHURCHYARD. © 2003 by Don Nigro. Reprinted by permission of the author and Samuel French, Inc. 45 W. 25 St., New York, NY 10010. Published by Samuel French, Inc. in *DeFlores and Other Plays*. Contact Samuel French, Inc. for performance rights.

DOCTOR FAUSTUS. © 2003 by Don Nigro. Reprinted by permission of the author and Samuel French, Inc., 45 W. 25 St., New York, NY 10010. Published in *DeFlores and Other Plays*. Contact Samuel French, Inc. for performance rights.

THE FACULTY ROOM. © 2003 by Bridget Carpenter. Reprinted by permission of Morgan Jenness, Helen Merrill Artists Ltd., 295 Lafayette St., New York, NY 10012, to whom inquiries may be addressed pertaining to performance rights. Published by Smith and Kraus, Inc. in *Humana Festival 2003: The Complete Plays*.

EIGHT DAYS (BACKWARDS). © 2003 by Jeremy Dobrish. Reprinted by permission of the author. All inquiries should be addressed to Peter Hagan, The Gersh Agency, 41 Madison Ave., New York, NY 10010.

THE FOURTH WALL. © 1996, 2003 by A. R. Gurney. Reprinted by permission of the William